The Pinel Family

From France to Brazil

Ronilda Pinel de Sousa Shomberg

ISBN 10: 1492766844
ISBN-13: 978-1492766841

PREFACE

This book was created to preserve the genealogical information and documentation collected over the last seven years regarding the descendants of Scipion Pinel.

It is not the purpose of this book to reprint all the information that is otherwise available in other family trees, internet, books and etc, but instead to document my family history to the generations to come. It does not cover all the descendants of Scipion Pinel only the seven generations leading to my mother's family. You are urged to read all the available material, learn as much as possible, and fill in the information of the next generations leading to you. Two extra pages has been added at the end of the book for this purpose.

Every effort has been made to make this book as complete and as accurate as possible. However, there may be mistakes, both typographical and in content. Therefore, this book should be used only as a guide and inspiration, not as the ultimate source of all the information related to the Pinel family.

Ronilda Pinel de Sousa Shomberg
NY, June 2013

"How will our children know who they are if they do not know where they came from."

To my children and grandchildren:

Ernest R (Pinel de Sousa) Vega
Grace R (Pinel de Sousa) Vega
Shawn M (Pinel de Sousa Vega) Clancy
Jillian R (Pinel de Sousa Vega) Clancy

CONTENTS

ACKNOWLEDGMENTS

I have not attempted to cite in the text all the authorities and sources consulted in the preparation of this book. To do so would require more space than is available. The list would include departments of various governments, libraries, periodicals and many individuals.

Numerous people contributed to this book. Distant cousins provided much needed information even though their names may not be included on the tree due to the seven generations limit I imposed on myself.

A special thanks to the cousins who helped me when I felt I could not move forward (or backwards).

Lucy Lupia Pinel Balthazar
Levy de Almeida Junior
Aladim Pinel
Paule Valet

1

WHAT IS IN A NAME?

I purchased the following Family Name History from the Historical Research Center in 1994. Although there are many versions of the Pinel name History, Coat of Arms, etc, I thought this would be a good curiosity item to start with. It says:

"The French surname Pinel is classified as being of local origin. Location names are family names that derive either from a feature of the location of the home of the first bearer of the name, or is the name of the town or village of the original bearer of the name.

In some cases, a location name makes reference to a house, which was distinguished by a sign or engraving usually placed above the door.

In this case, the name Pinel identify, in principle, a man who lived in a place or found himself surrounded by one or more pines. The name Pinel, is a derivation of the name "Pine", which was taken from the French word of the same spelling that comes from the Latin "pinus".

The main variants of the name Pinel are Pin and Dupin. It is said that the use of hereditaries names in France appeared in the fifteenth century.

This process spans over two hundred years, since the custom to have a name passed to the next generation already begun in the thirteenth century. A reference to the old name or a variation of that name is the register of baptism of Guillaume Pinel, son of Jean Baptiste Pinel and Catherine Houdan, which took place in Dordogne, in 1676.

On the other hand, in a French armorial, are recorded three different families, who founded their ancestral homes in the regions of Brittany, Normandy and Languedoc. Research is still ongoing, and the name could have been documented earlier than the date mentioned here. Notable figures who have that name is the French doctor Philippe Pinel, born near

Gibronges, today Jonquieres (1745-1826)"

Arms: Azure, three green pine cones
Interpretation: Azure (blue) signifies loyalty and truth and Vert (green), hope and joy.
Crest: Three ostrich feathers
Origin: France

According to the description the following would be a good representation of our Coat of Arms:

Figure 1
Blue background, 3 green pine cones and 3 ostrich feathers a top.

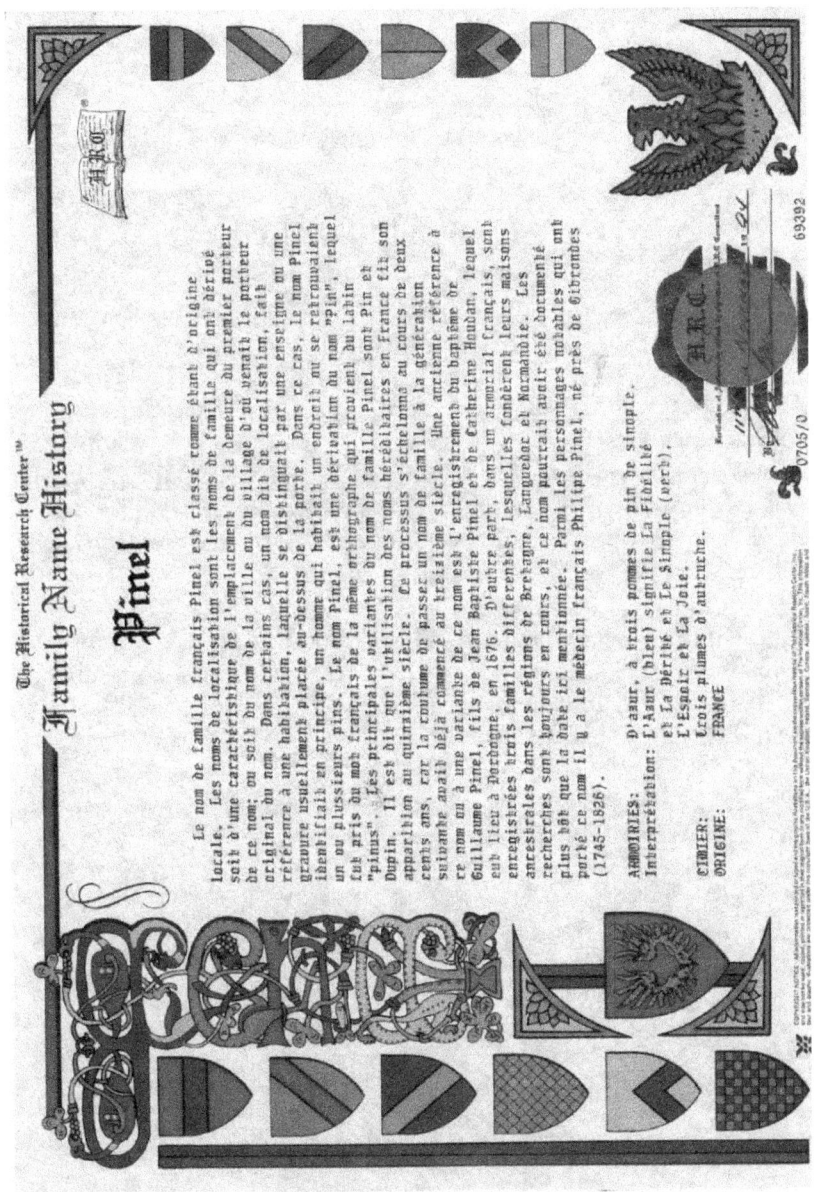

Figure 2

SCIPION PINEL
And his descendants

Generation 1

1.   **SCIPION[1] PINEL** was born in 1660 in Saint-Paul-Cap-de-Joux, France. He died on 04 August 1714 (buried on the 5th) in Saint-Paul-Cap-de-Joux, France. He married **SUSANNE OLIENE**. She was born about 1670 in Saint-Paul-Cap-de-Joux, France. Her date of death is unknown but estimated between 1704, after the birth of her last child, and before 1714, death of Scipion.

All births, deaths, marriage information for 1674-1792 collected from archivesenligne.tarn.fr. Note that 1680-1691 is not available for St. Paul Cap de Joux parish and 1679-1733 is not available for St Andre D'Alayrac parish.

Scipion and Susanne were godparents/witnesses of many of the births and marriages registered in St Paul.

1694

1696

Scipion's death was entered in Saint-Paul's church register and witnessed by Pierre Martin. Side note says "see wife's death at Lavaur".

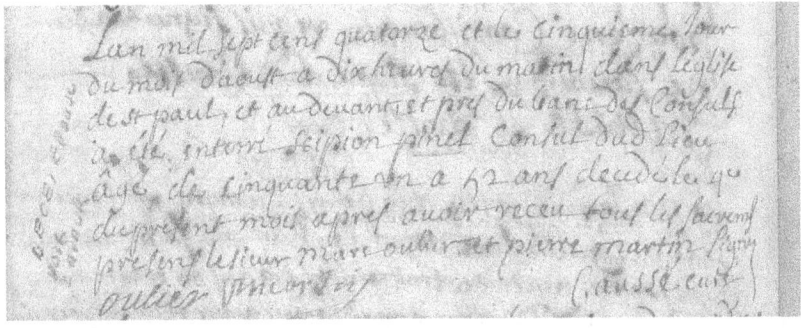

The existence of Susanne Oliene: is proved by the many entrances in the registry of their children baptism: 1E_266_001_4 Bapteme Saint-Paul 1704-1726 communale http://archives.tarn.fr

Scipion Pinel and Susanne Oliene had the following children, *(generation 2)*:

2.   i.   **BARTHELEMÍ OLIENE[2] PINEL** (Scipion[1]) was born in 1690 in Saint-Paul-Cap-de-Joux, France. He died on 13 February 1758 in Saint-Paul-Cap-de-Joux, France. He married **MARIE ESCRIBE**. She was born in 1696 in Saint-Paul-Cap-de-Joux, France. She died on 04 September 1745 in Saint-Paul-Cap-de-Joux, France.

2.   ii.   JEANNE OLIENE[2] PINEL (Scipion[1]) was born in 1693 in Saint-Paul-Cap-de-Joux, France (earliest date for age of innocence). She died on 28 May 1699 in Saint-Paul-Cap-de-Joux, France (death at age of innocence).

2.   iii.   BERNARD OLIENE[2] PINEL (Scipion[1]) was born on 25 November 1694 in Saint-Paul-Cap-de-Joux, France. His baptism was recorded in the Saint-Paul Parish Register on November 28. Godparents: Bernard Sabatien and Marie Barla du Ladite

2. iv. MARIANNE OLIENE[2] PINEL (Scipion[1]) was born on 22 March 1697 in Saint-Paul-Cap-de-Joux, France. She was baptized on March 25 and the fact recorded in the Saint-Paul Parish. Her Godfather was her brother Barthelemí Pinel and Godmother was Susanne de la Vale.

2. v. NOE OLIENE[2] PINEL (Scipion[1]) was born on the 28 of March, 1700 in Saint-Paul-Cap-de-Joux, France and baptized in their Parish on 2nd of April. His Godparents: Barthelemí, brother and Jeanne, sister. He died on 23 April 1701 and was buried at the cemetery of Saint-Paul-Cap-de-Joux Parish, France.

2. vi. MARIE OLIENE[2] PINEL (Scipion[1]) was born on 17 August 1702 and baptized on August 20th in Saint-Paul-Cap-de-Joux, France Parish, her Godfather was Barthelemí Oliene Pinel, her brother and Godmother: Madame Antoine Pech. She died on 14 July 1703 and was buried on the 15th at the Saint-Paul-Cap-de-Joux Parish Cemetery, France.

2. vii. MARGUERITTE OLIENE[2] PINEL (Scipion[1]) was born on 03 July 1704 and baptized on the 5th of July in the Parish of Saint-Paul-Cap-de-Joux, France. Godfather: Jean Oliene, cousin and Godmother: Catherine Martine, cousin

Generation 2

2.   **BARTHELEMÍ OLIENE[2] PINEL** (Scipion[1]) was born in 1690 in Saint-Paul-Cap-de-Joux, France. He died on 13 February 1758 in Saint-Paul-Cap-de-Joux, France. He married **MARIE ESCRIBE**. She was born in 1696 in Saint-Paul-Cap-de-Joux, France. She died on 04 September 1745 in Saint-Paul-Cap-de-Joux, France.

Marie Escribe had alternate spelling of her name: Escirve, Escribe or Scribe. From: http://gw1.geneanet.org

Barthelemí Pinel and Marie Escribe moved from Saint-Paul-Cap-de-Joux to Damiatte (just across the river Agout), France. Although none were born in Damiatte, marriage and death registers shows the existence of their other children.

Figure 3

Barthelemí Oliene Pinel and Marie Escribe had the following children *(generation 3)*:

3.   i. HIPPOLITE ESCRIBE[3] PINEL (Barthelemí Oliene[2], Scipion[1]) was born on 27 August 1711 and baptized on the 30th of August in the Parish of Saint-Paul-Cap-de-Joux, France. Her Godparents were Scipion Pinel, grandfather and Hippolite Deferine, aunt. She died on 04

March 1791 in Damiatte, Tarn, France.

She married JEAN DURAND, son of Pierre Durand and Marie on 19 February 1737 in Église Saint Martin, Damiatte, Tarn, France. He was born on 28 March 1711 and baptized on the 30th of the month in Damiatte, Tarn, France. He died in Sarger.

3.   ii. JEAN ESCRIBE[3] PINEL (Barthelemí Oliene[2], Scipion[1]) was born on 8 January 1713 and baptized on the 10th of the same month in Saint-Paul-Cap-de-Joux, France. His Godparents were Jean Miguel de Daussie and Susanne Oliene, grandmother. His uncle Bernard Pinel was a witness. His date of death is unknown.   He married MARIE MAVIES.

3.   iii. JEANNE   ESCRIBE[3]   PINEL   (Barthelemí Oliene[2], Scipion[1]) was born on 10 March 1714 and baptized on the 15th of March in Saint-Paul-Cap-de-Joux, France. Godfather: Marc Oliene, uncle. Godmother: Jeanne Pinel. Witnesses: the grandfather Scipion Pinel and Antoine Caussé. Her date of death is presumed to be before 1723 when another child was born and named Jeanne..

3.   iv.   MARIE ESCRIBE[3] PINEL (Barthelemí Oliene[2], Scipion[1]) was born on 04 June 1715 and baptized on the 10[Th] of the same month in the Parish of Saint-Paul-Cap-de-Joux, France. Godfather: Bernard Pinel, uncle. Godmother: Marie Garthe and Witnesses: Marc Oliene, consul of Saint-Paul and the Noble Marc Antoine Dupuy. Her date of death is unknown.

3.   v.   **PHILIPPE FRANÇOIS ESCRIBE[3] PINEL** (Barthelemí Oliene[2], Scipion[1]) was born on the last day of May (31st) and baptized on 07 June 1716 in the Parish of Saint-Paul-Cap-de-Joux, France. He died on 01 Oct 1793 in Saint-Paul-Cap-de-Joux, France. He married ÉLISABETH DUPUY, daughter of Charles Dupuy and Margueritte Bugarel on 11 February 1744 in Saint Andre, Tarn, France. She was born in 1722 in Saint Andre, Tarn, France. She died in 1757.

1716 Baptism of Philippe François Escribe Pinel – Saint-Paul Parish Register

His Godfather was Philippe Oliene, grand-uncle and his Godmother was Jeanne Oliene, widow grandmother of the baptized (although Scipion's wife was Susanne Oliene maybe a misunderstanding at the time). The witnesses: Pierre Martin and Jean Antoine Caussé

3. vi. CLAIRE ESCRIBE[3] PINEL (Barthelemí Oliene[2], Scipion[1]) was born on 13 February 1718 and baptized on the 14th, in Parish of Saint-Paul-Cap-de-Joux, France. Godfather: Jean Rigoud, a farmer of Pecharnié. Godmother: Marie Lengone

3. vii. MAGDALEINE ESCRIBE[3] PINEL (Barthelemí Oliene[2], Scipion[1]) was born on 7 February 1719 and baptized on the 12th of the month in Saint-Paul-Cap-de-Joux, France. Godfather: Guilhaume Fienge, baker of Lavaur. Godmother: Magdaleine, her cousin. She died on 27 September 1719 and buried on the 29th in the Parish cemetery of Saint-Paul-Cap-de-Joux, France.

3. viii. MARIANNE ESCRIBE[3] PINEL (Barthelemí Oliene[2], Scipion[1]) was born on 09 February 1719 and baptized on the 11th of the month in Saint-Paul-Cap-de-Joux, France (twin of Magdaleine?). Her godparents were Jean Antoine Caussé and Hypolithe Escribe, aunt.
3. ix. CHARLES ESCRIBE[3] PINEL (Barthelemí Oliene[2],

Scipion[1]) was born on 27 April 1721 and baptized on the 1st of May in Saint-Paul-Cap-de-Joux, France. Godfather: Noble Charles Dupuy. Godmother: Noble Marianne Dupuy. Witness: Noble Pierre de Raimond

He married Marguerite Ribairan on 13 February 1760 in Damiatte, Tarn, France. She was born on 03 March 1729 in Damiatte, France (baptized at Saint-Martin de Damiatte). She died on 06 May 1777 in Damiatte, Tarn, France.

3.   x.   JEANNE   ESCRIBE[3]   PINEL   (Barthelemí Oliene[2], Scipion[1]) was born on 02 May 1723 and baptized in the 7th of the month in Saint Paul-Cap-de-Joux, Tarn FR. Godfather was Jacques Pech and godmother was Hipolite Pinel

3.   xi.   MARGUERITTE   ESCRIBE3   PINEL (Barthelemí Oliene[2], Scipion[1]) was born on 17 April 1725 in Saint-Paul-Cap-de-Joux, France. Her date of death is unknown.

3.   xii. ANNE ESCRIBE[3] PINEL (Barthelemí Oliene[2], Scipion[1]) was born in 1740 in Saint Paul-Cap-de-Joux, Tarn FR. Her date of death is unknown. She married JEAN LOUIS RIBAYRAN (RIBAIRAN) on 13 February 1760 in Damiatte, Tarn, France. His date of death is unknown.

Generation 3

3.   HIPPOLITE ESCRIBE[3] PINEL (Barthelemí Oliene[2], Scipion[1]) was born on 27 August 1711 in Saint-Paul-Cap-de-Joux, France. She died on 04 March 1791 in Damiatte, Tarn, France. She married JEAN DURAND, son of Pierre Durand and Marie on 19 February 1737 in Église Saint Martin, Damiatte, Tarn, France. He was born on 28 March 1711 in Damiatte, Tarn, France. He died in Sarger.

> 1711 Baptism of Jean Durand – Damiatte Parish Register Godparents Alexi Guetolle e Marie Duran

> 1737 Marriage of Hippolite Pinel and Jean Durand – Saint-Martin Parish Register (Damiatte). Witness: Pierre Duran, father of the groom and Barthelemí Pinel, father of the bride

> 1791 Death of Hippolite Pinel Durand – Damiatte Parish Register. Notes from register: Age 80. Spouse of Jean Durand (meaning husband Jean still alive). Witness: Gaspard Jauce and Barthelemí Poutton

Jean Durand and Hippolite Escribe Pinel had the following child (*generation 4*):

> 4.   i.   MARIE JEANNE FRANÇOISE PINEL[4] DURAND (Hippolite Escribe[3], Barthelemí Oliene[2], Scipion[1]) was born on 12 August 1741 and baptized on the 15th of the month in Damiatte, Tarn, France. Godfather was François G. Durand (priest and vicar of St Salvy de Siac) her uncle, and godmother was her aunt Claire Pinel. Witness was grandfather Pierre Durand. Her date of death is unknown.

3.   JEAN ESCRIBE[3] PINEL (Barthelemí Oliene[2], Scipion[1]) was born on 10 January 1713 in Saint-Paul-Cap-de-Joux, France. His date of death is unknown. He married MARIE.

Jean Escribe Pinel and Marie had the following child (*generation 4*):

4.   i.   MARGUERITTE[4] PINEL (Jean[3], Barthelemí Oliene[2], Scipion[1]) was born on 30 August 1754 and baptized on the 1st of September in Saint Paul-Cap-de-Joux, Tarn FR. Godfather: Antoine Frouvier. Godmother: Margueritte Endrieu

3.   **PHILIPPE FRANÇOIS ESCRIBE[3] PINEL** (Barthelemí Oliene[2], Scipion[1]) was born on 07 June 1716 in Saint-Paul-Cap-de-Joux, France. He died on 01 Oct 1793 in Saint-Paul-Cap-de-Joux, France. He married ÉLISABETH DUPUY, daughter of Charles Dupuy and Margueritte Bugarel on 11 February 1744 in Saint Andre, Tarn, France. She was born in 1722 in Saint Andre, Tarn, France. She died in 1757.

Philippe François Escribe Pinel signature as godfather in 1756.

"In 1744, the father, Philippe Pinel, married Elizabeth Dupuy, and a year later their first child, Philippe, was born. Of the seven Pinel children only four survived : Philippe, Charles, Louis, and Jean-Pierre".
From a book by Bernard Mackler, 1968.

1744 Marriage of Philippe François Pinel and Élisabeth Dupuy - Saint Andre Parish Register, three pages

First Page

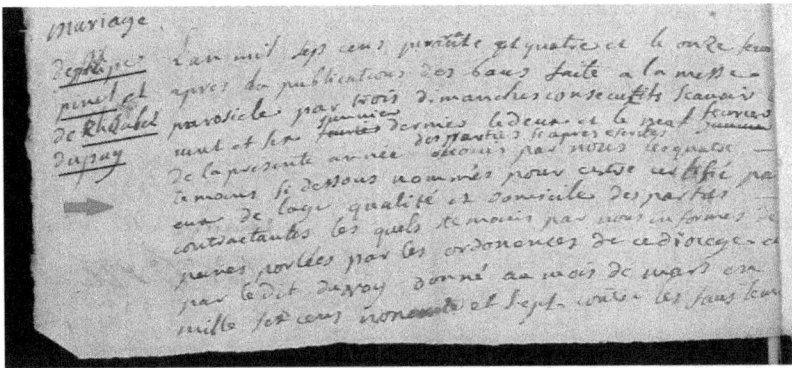

Second page

Last page

The last page shows signatures of Bernard Pinel, master baker of Lavaur and Jean Durand, master responsible for the Parish of Damiatte, diocese of Castres. Pierre Bugarel was a witness.

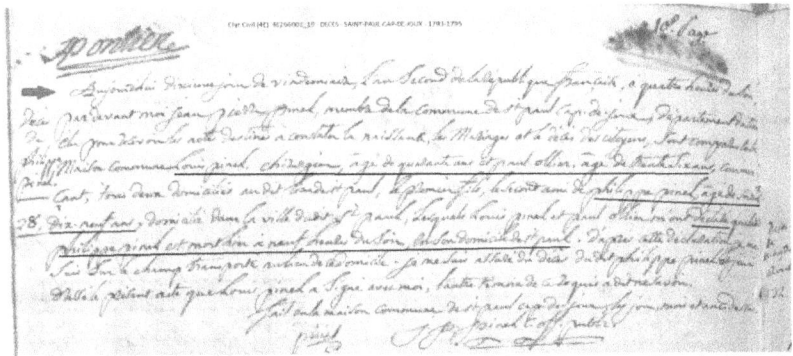

His death in 1793 was declared by his son, Louis Pinel, surgeon, age 40.

(See Élisabeth Bugarel Dupuy family line in Chapter 3)

Philippe François Escribe Pinel and Élisabeth Dupuy had the following children *(generation 4)*:

4.　i. **PHILIPPE DUPUY⁴ PINEL** (Philippe François Escribe[3], Barthelemí Oliene[2], Scipion[1]) was born on 20 April 1745 in Saint Andre, Tarn, France. He died on 25 Oct 1826 in Paris, Paris, Ile-de-France, France.

He married (1) **JEANNE FRANÇOISE VINCENT**, daughter of Jean Vincent and Jeanne Françoise Gindre on 20 March 1792 in Paris, Ile-de-France, France. She was born on 03 July 1768 in Geruge, Franche-Comté, France. She died in 1812.

He married (2) MARIE-MADELEINE JACQUELIN LAVALLÉE on 25 November 1815. She was born in Saint-Paul-Cap-de-Joux, France. Her date of death　　　is　　　unknown.

4.　ii. CHARLES DUPUY⁴ PINEL (Philippe François Escribe[3], Barthelemí Oliene[2], Scipion[1]) was baptized on 13 February 1748 in Saint-Paul-Cap-de-Joux, France. Godparents were Jean Pinel and Marianne Dupuy. He married JEANNE ARQUIE.

4. iii. FRANÇOIS DUPUY[4] PINEL (Philippe François Escribe[3], Barthelemí Oliene[2], Scipion[1]) was baptized on 26 January 1749 in Saint-Paul-Cap-de-Joux, France. Godfather: François Durand and Godmother: Claire Pinel

He died on 26 December 1749 in Saint Andre, Tarn, France.

4. iv. PIERRE-LOUIS DUPUY[4] PINEL (Philippe François Escribe[3], Barthelemí Oliene[2], Scipion[1]) was born in 1752 in Saint-Paul-Cap-de-Joux, France. His date of death is unknown. He married LOUISE GUILLEMAND.

4. v. CHARLE DUPUY[4] PINEL (Philippe François Escribe[3], Barthelemí Oliene[2], Scipion[1]) was baptized on 18 November 1753 in Saint-Paul-Cap-de-Joux, France. Godfather: Charles Pinel, uncle and Godmother: Anne Pinel, aunt. Her date of death is unknown.

4. vi. JEAN PIERRE DUPUY[4] PINEL (Philippe François Escribe[3], Barthelemí Oliene[2], Scipion[1]) was baptized on 07 October, 1755 in Saint-Paul-Cap-de-Joux, France. His godparents were Jean Durand and Élisabeth Lafend. He married MARIANNE OULIAC.

4. vii. MARIE DUPUY[4] PINEL (Philippe François Escribe[3], Barthelemí Oliene[2], Scipion[1]) was baptized on 27 November 1757 in Saint-Paul-Cap-de-Joux, France. Godfather: Philippe Pinel, brother and Godmother: Marie Duran. Her date of death is unknown.

3. CHARLES ESCRIBE[3] PINEL (Barthelemí Oliene[2], Scipion[1]) was born on 27 April 1721 in Saint-Paul-Cap-de-Joux, France. He married MARGUERITE RIBAIRAN on 13 February 1760 in Damiatte, Tarn, France with Pierre Jauxion and Jean Durand as witness.

Margueritte was born on 03 March 1729 in Damiatte, France (baptized at Saint-Martin de Damiatte). She died on 06 May

1777 in Damiatte, Tarn, France.

Baptism Notes for Marguerite Ribairan:
Parents: Jean Ribairan and Marie Recfel
Godfather Ettiene Recfel
Godmother: Margueritte Ribairand

Death Notes:
Wife of Charles Pinel, surgeon. died at age of 45 (does not fit in with birth date, should be 48).

Charles Escribe Pinel and Marguerite Ribairan had the following children (*generation 4*):

4.   i.   ANNE RIBAYRAN[4] PINEL (Charles Escribe[3], Barthelemí Oliene[2], Scipion[1]) was baptized on 28 November 1765 in Damiatte, Tarn, France. Godfather: Philippe Pinel, surgeon de St Paul. Godmother: Anne Ribairan, a parishioner. Her Father was absent. Her date of death is unknown.

4.   ii.   MARIE RIBAYRAN[4] PINEL (Charles Escribe[3], Barthelemí Oliene[2], Scipion[1]) was baptized on 15 June 1767 in Damiatte, Tarn, France. Godfather: Pierre Jauzion. Godmother: Marie Vocaxe. Her date of death is unknown.

4.   iii.   JEAN RIBAYRAN[4] PINEL (Charles Escribe[3], Barthelemí Oliene[2], Scipion[1]) was born on 04 September 1769 in Damiatte, Tarn, France.

Baptism Notes:
Godfather: Jean Durand
Godmother: Marie Marty, of St Paul

3

ÉLISABETH BUGAREL DUPUY
And Her Ancestors

1. **ANTOINE[1] BUGAREL (BUGARD)** was born in 1655 in Saint-Julien Du Puy, Tarn, FR (at a small village near Graulhet - Église Saint-Julien du Puy). He died on 20 Oct 1729 in Saint-Julien Du Puy, Tarn, FR. He married **CATHERINE FABRE** on 05 January 1682 in Saint-Julien Du Puy, Tarn, FR. She died on 25 May 1693 in Saint-Julien Du Puy, Tarn, FR.

Antoine Bugarel (Bugard) and Catherine Fabre had the following children:

> 2   i.   MARIE[2] BUGAREL was born on 30 November 1691 in Saint-Julien Du Puy, Tarn, FR. She died on 14 January 1782 in Saint-Julien Du Puy, Tarn, FR.

> 2.   ii.   MARIE THÉRÈSE[2] BUGAREL was born on 16 Oct 1692 in Saint-Julien Du Puy, Tarn, FR. She died on 25 November1702 in Saint-Julien Du Puy, Tarn, FR.

> 2.   iii.   PIERRE[2] BUGAREL was born on 01 November 1689 in Saint-Julien Du Puy, Tarn, FR. He died on 29 Oct 1749 in Saint-Julien Du Puy, Tarn, FR. He married Anne Marie DURAND on 21 November 1718 in Dénat, Tarn, Midi-Pyrénées, France (L'Église de Dénat, corner of Rue des Remparts and Rue de Goy). She was born on 07 Oct 1698 in Dénat, Tarn, Midi-Pyrénées, France. She died on 15 Oct 1768 in Saint Julien-du-Puy, Lautrec, Castres, Tarn, FR.

3. iv. **MARGUERITTE² BUGAREL** was born in 1682 in Saint-Julien Du Puy, Tarn, FR. She died on 26 June 1766 in Saint Andre, Tarn, France. She married Charles Dupuy on 16 January 1719. He was born in 1683 in Saint-Paul-Cap-de-Joux, France. He died on 22 November 1751 in Saint Andre, Tarn, France (age 68).

Generation 2

2. **MARGUERITTE² BUGAREL** (Antoine¹ Bugard (Bugarel)) was born in 1682 in Saint-Julien Du Puy, Tarn, FR. She married **CHARLES DUPUY** on 16 January 1719. He was born in 1683 in Saint-Paul-Cap-de-Joux, France. He was buried on 22 November 1751 in Saint Andre, Tarn, France (age 68).

Margueritte Bugarel death notes from Parish Register:
Widow of Messier Dupuy, Surgeon. Witness: Jean Baptist Bugarel, vicar. Age senviron = 84 (approximate age =84)

Charles Dupuy and Margueritte Bugarel had the following children:

3. i. **ÉLISABETH³ BUGAREL DUPUY** (Margueritte², Antoine¹) was born in 1722 in Saint Andre, Tarn, France. She died in 1757. She married **PHILIPPE FRANÇOIS (ESCRIBE) PINEL**, son of Barthelemí Oliene Pinel and Marie Escribe on 11 February 1744 in Saint Andre, Tarn, France. He was born on 07 June 1716 in Saint-Paul-Cap-de-Joux, France. He died on 01 Oct 1793 in Saint-Paul-Cap-de-Joux, France.

3 ii. MARIANNE³ BUGAREL DUPUY (Margueritte², Antoine¹) was born in 1725 in Saint Andre, Tarn, France. She died on 28 July 1779 in Saint Andre, Tarn, France. She married Alexis Bastier on 30 July 1749. He was born in 1719 in Saint-Paul-Cap-de-Joux, France.

4

PHILIPPE DUPUY PINEL
Generation 4

Figure 4

4.   **PHILIPPE DUPUY[4] PINEL** (Philippe François Escribe[3], Barthelemí Oliene[2], Scipion[1]) was born on 20 April 1745 in Saint Andre, Tarn, France. He died on 25 Oct 1826 in Paris, Paris, Ile-de-France.

He married (first) **JEANNE FRANÇOISE VINCENT**, daughter of Jean Vincent and Jeanne Françoise Gindre on 20 March 1792 in Paris, Ile-de-France, France. She was born on 03 July 1768 in Geruge, Franche-Comté, France. She died in 1812. (*see her family line in Chapter 5*)

Notes for his marriage to Jeanne Françoise:

Philippe wrote his father a letter requesting permission to marry

21

From the book «Philippe Pinel et son œuvré au point de vue de la médecine mentale » By René Semelaigne

Page 157

«   …sens très vivement la nécessite de m'unir avec une personne qui soit un autre moi-même et a laquelle je puisse me confier entièrement,

«   Sois bien persuade que je ne m'y suis détermine qu'après une réflexion et après avoir tout balancer. je prie mon père de vouloir bien m'envoyer tout de suite son consentement a peu prés dans la forme qui suit:

«   Je donne mon consentement pur et simple au mariage de mon fils aine, Philippe Pinel, avec demoiselle Jeanne Vincent, fille légitime de feu Jean Vincent et de Françoise Gindre, habitants de Gevingey, département du Jura, entendant que ce mariage sera contracte suivant les formes civiles et ecclésiastiques.

< Fait a Saint Paul, ce... >

Je te prie de m'envoyer par la même lettre un extrait mortuaire de ma mère qui me devient aussi nécessaire. «

"…I feel very strongly the need to unite with a person who is like myself and one that I can confide entirely,

After reflecting and balancing the facts, I am convinced and determined of it. I pray for my father to send me immediately consent roughly in the following form:

"I give my consent to outright marriage of my eldest son, Philippe Pinel, with Miss Jeanne Vincent, legitimate daughter of the late Jean Vincent and Françoise Gindre, residents Gevingey, department of Jura, understanding that this wedding will be contracted following civil and ecclesiastical forms.

<Signed in Saint Paul, this ... >

I beg you to send me with the same letter my mother's death certificate which is also necessary."

He married (second) MARIE-MADELEINE JACQUELIN LAVALLÉE on 25 November 1815. She was born in Saint-Paul-Cap-de-Joux, France. Her date of death is unknown.

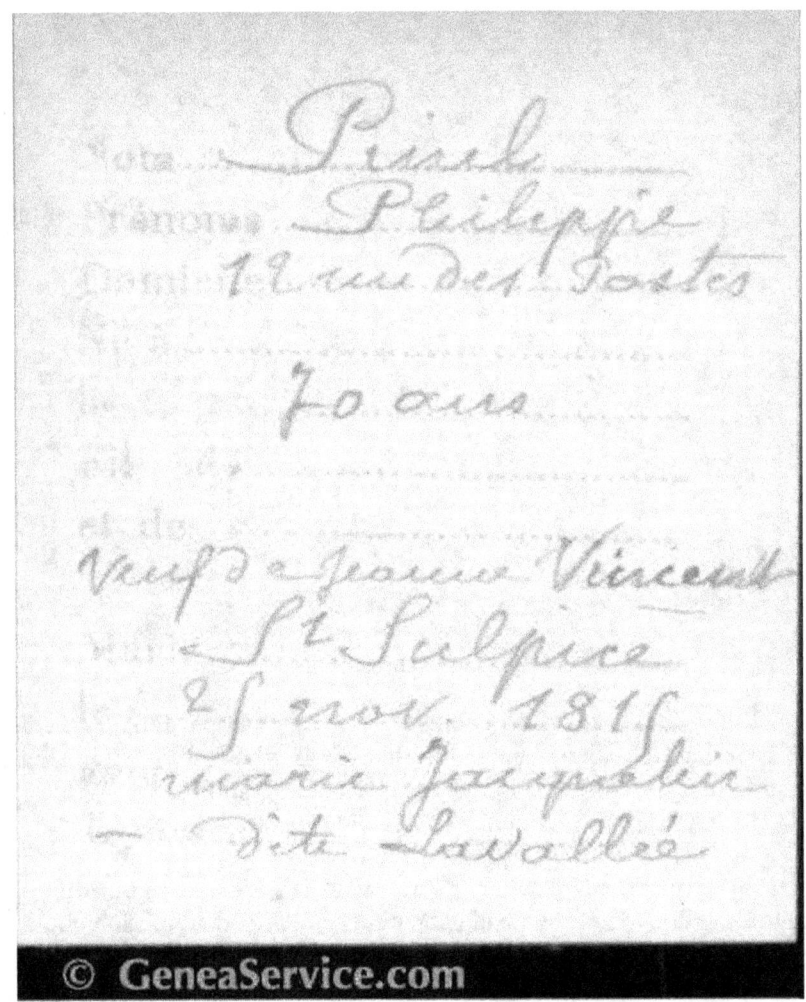

Philippe Pinel was born April 20, 1745, during a temporary absence of his mother from St. Paul, at St. Andre, France. His father was a country doctor, with five children to support, whose early education he cared for by hiring a private tutor.

Notes from baptism register: son of Philippe Pinel, master surgeon and Élisabeth Dupuy. Godfather: Barthelemì Pinel, paternal grandfather. Godmother Margueritte Bugarel, grandmother. Witness: Charles Dupuy, master surgeon.

In personal appearance Pinel was of small stature, but well proportioned and of strong constitution. He had a broad, high, and prominent forehead, black hair and aquiline nose, rounded chin, small mouth, and a sweet and affable smile. His character was a mingling of benevolence and reflection, his bearing reserved and austere. " In seeing Pinel," says Guillaume Dupuytren, " one would have imagined he was looking at a Greek sage. His nature was tender and sensitive. He loved beauty and sublimity. He always kept up his taste for poetry, and was passionately in love

with the masterpieces of antiquity." Indeed, his biographer narrates that his poetic sensibility was so extreme that, in discoursing of a fate so fraught with glory and misery as that of the Greek poet Sappho, he would sob with emotion. .
by
THE AMERICAN JOURNAL OF Psychiatry PUBLISHED UNDER THE AUSPICES OF THE AMERICAN MEDICO-PSYCHOLOGICAL ASSOCIATION
Editors Henry M. Hurd, M. D. G. Alder Blumer, M. D. Edward N. Brush, M. D. J. Montgomery Mosher, M. D.
VOLUME LV
_' The care of the human mind is the most noble branch of medicine.'-Grotius. BALTIMORE THE JOHNS HOPKINS PRESS 1898-99.

Education

High School: Lavaur School, Lavaur, France
University: Collège Les Clauzades, Lavaur, France
Medical School: MD, Collège de l'Esquille, Toulouse (1773)

Work

Teacher: Medical Pathology, University of Paris (1794-95)
Professor: Medical Pathology, University of Paris (1795-1826)

Asylum de Bicêtre (hospital for men)Superintendent (1792-94)

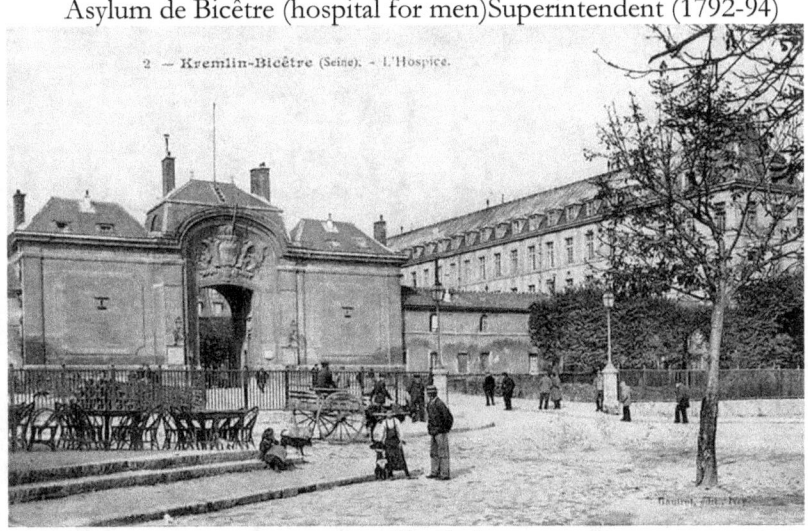

Figure 5

Hospice de la Salpêtrière (hospital for women)Superintendent (1794-1826) – Figure 6

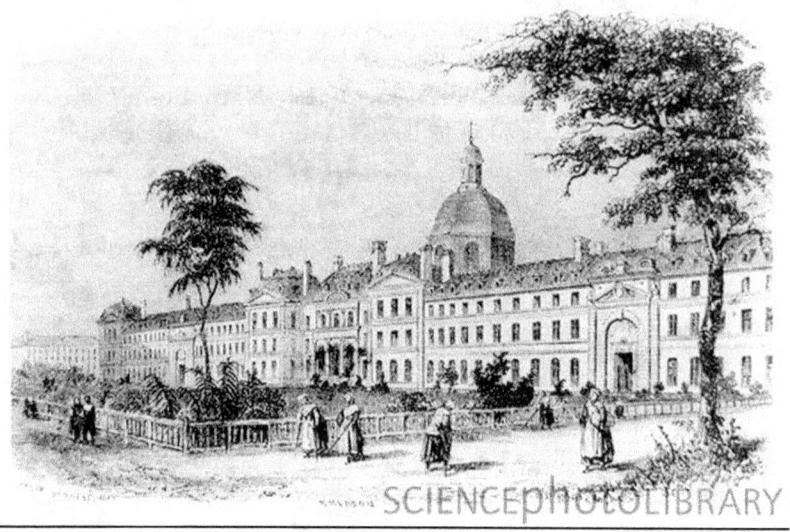

French Academy of Medicine 1820
French Academy of Sciences 1804
Honors
He was made Chevalier of the Legion d'Honneur in 1804.

Figure 7

Famous French doctor, born on 20 April 1745, at Schloss Rascas, commune of Saint-André (Tarn), died in Paris on 26 October 1826. Son and grandson of doctors, he was admitted to the doctorate at Toulouse in 1773. He started by giving lessons in mathematics and translated several scientific works in English to French. Finally he applies himself to the study of insanity since 1784.

His Traité médico-philosophique sur l'aliénation mentale was the starting point for all work performed thereafter in this area.
Author: Pinel, Philippe, 1745-1826
Subject: Psychiatry -- Early works to 1900; Psychiatry -- France
Publisher: Paris, J.A. Brosson

For a few years after 1805 Pinel was a personal physician for Napoleon Bonaparte, but rejected the offer of becoming court physician, as this would take his efforts away from his work as a clinical physician, scientist and teacher. Pinel was elected to the Académie des Sciences in 1804 and was a member of the Academy of Medicine from its founding in 1820.

PARIS ANCIEN

(Décès) VILLE D E *P.........* 12e

NOM ....*Pinel*........

Prénoms ....

Profession ....*Philippe*....

Date du Décès .....*25 Octob. 1826*

Age ou date de naissance *81 ans*...

Lieu de naissance ....

Domicile ...*12 Bd de l Hopital*

Prénoms du père ....

Prénoms et noms de la mère ....

Marié à ....

Divorcé ou Veuf de ......*Vincent*....

Parenté des déclarants et renseignements sur le degré de parenté des héritiers que vous pourriez connaître.

M Pinel petite fille

.....*155 Av d Eylau*......

....

....

Death Notes:
Widow of Vincent. Declared by Marie Pinel, daughter resident at 155 Av d'Eylou

Burial: Cimetière du Père Lachaise, Paris, Ile-de-France, France
Plot: Division #18, 2nd row, U, 23 - Figure 8

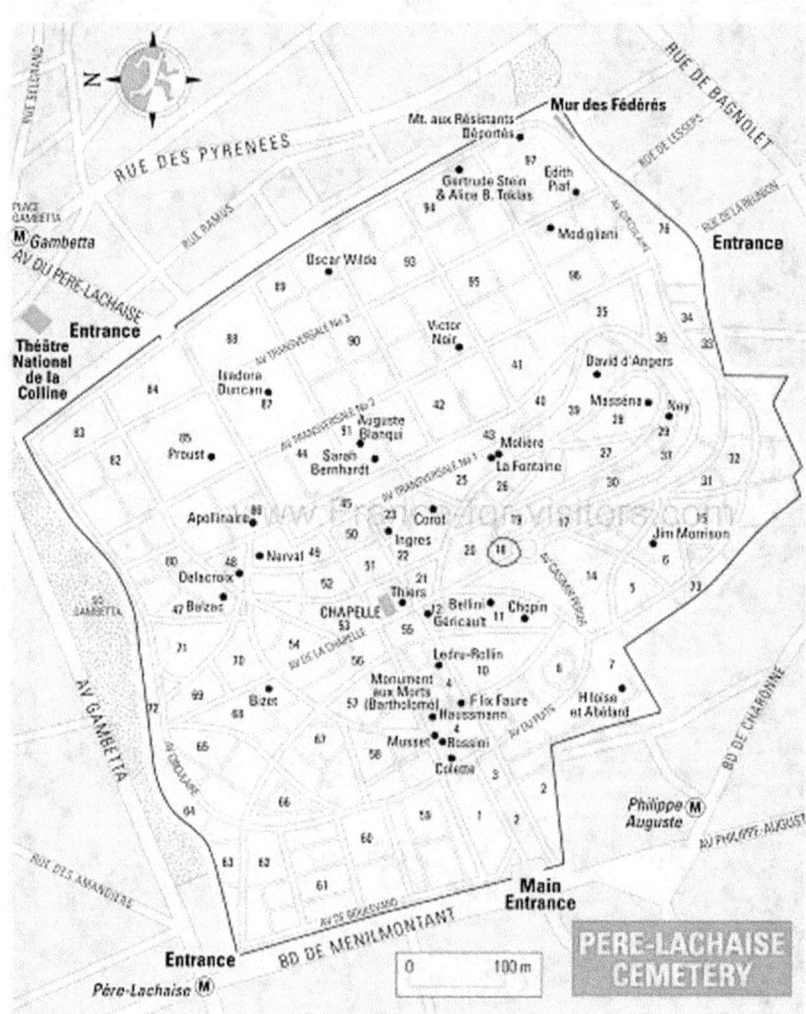

Père Lachaise map, circle shows division#18 where Pinel is buried.
http://france-for-visitors.com/

The commemorative coin was minted by the Medallic Art Co. N.Y in 1970. and was cast in bronze. The reverse of the medal holds the inscription "Unchaining the insane" and shows an image of three men releasing a mental patient from chains on his wrists. The obverse contains a bust of Pinel with his name, birth and death dates, and the inscription "French Psychiatrist" surrounding the image. The medal measures 1 ¾ inches in diameter.

Figure 9

An image of 'the father of modern psychiatry' in the courtyard of the old stables block in the grounds of the Royal Edinburgh Hospital.

Pinel Head Sculpture at Edinburg Hospital – Figure 10

Statue of psychiatrist Philippe Pinel in front of the entrance of the Hôspital de la Salpêtrière in Paris, France.

Figure 11

Pinel commemorative stamp

Figure 12

Pinel street sign

Figure 13
located in the neighborhood of the Salpêtrière in
the 13th arrondissement of Paris .

Philippe Dupuy Pinel and Jeanne Françoise Vincent had the following children *(generation 5):*

Philippe with Scipion and Jeanne with Charles - 1807
painting by Julie Forestier
Figure 14

5.   i. **CHARLES VINCENT[5] PINEL** (Philippe Dupuy[4], Philippe François Escribe[3], Barthelemí Oliene[2], Scipion)was born on 27 April 1802 in Paris, Île-de-France, France. He died on 18 July 1871 in Nova Friburgo, Rio de Janeiro, BR (Paróquia São João Baptista). He married **MARIE CATHERINE RIME**, daughter of Felix Rime and Marie Veronique Tornare on 27 April 1835 in Nova Friburgo, Rio de Janeiro, BR. She was born in 1816 in Charmey, Fribourg, Switzerland (Saint Lawrence of Charmey). She died on 05 August 1890 in Nova Friburgo, Rio de Janeiro, BR.

5.   ii. SCIPION PHILIPPE VINCENT[5] PINEL(Philippe Dupuy 4, Philippe François Escribe[3], Barthelemí Oliene[2], Scipion) was born on 22 March 1795 in Paris, Ile-de-France, France. He died on 17 December 1859 in Paris, Ile-de-France, France. He married HARMONIE MARGUERITE LEFEBVRE on 03 April 1824 in Paris, Ile-de-France, France (St Jean-St François). She was born in Saint-Paul-Cap-de-Joux, France. Her date of death is unknown.

5.   iii.   MARIE[5] VINCENT[5] PINEL(Philippe Dupuy 4, Philippe François Escribe[3], Barthelemí Oliene[2], Scipion) was born in Paris, Ile-de-France, France. Her date of death is unknown.

4.   CHARLES DUPUY[4] PINEL (Philippe François Escribe[3], Barthelemí Oliene[2], Scipion) was born on 13 February 1748 in Saint-Paul-Cap-de-Joux, France. He married JEANNE ARQUIE.

> Baptism Notes:
> Godfather: Jean Pinel
> Godmother: Marianne Dupuy

> Charles Dupuy Pinel and Jeanne Arquie had the following children *(generation 5)*:

5.   i.   LOUISE HELIODORE ARQUIE[5] PINEL (Charles Dupuy[4], Philippe François Escribe[3], Barthelemí Oliene[2], Scipion) was born on 10 April 1790 in Saint Paul-Cap-de-Joux, Tarn FR.

Baptism Notes:
Godfather: Louis Pinel, surgeon
Godmother: Louise Guilidmam

5.   ii.   JEAN PIERRE FLORENTIN ARQUIE[5] PINEL
(Charles Dupuy[4], Philippe François Escribe[3], Barthelemí
Oliene[2], Scipion) was born on 23 January 1792 in Saint Paul-
Cap-de-Joux, Tarn FR.

Baptism Notes:
Godfather: Jean Pierre Pinel, cure de St Paul
Godmother: Marie Arquier

4.   PIERRE-LOUIS DUPUY[4] PINEL (Philippe François Escribe[3],
Barthelemí Oliene[2], Scipion[1]) was born in 1752 in Saint-Paul-Cap-de-
Joux, France. His date of death is unknown. He married LOUISE
GUILLEMAND.

Pierre-Louis Dupuy Pinel and Louise Guillemand had the
following children *(generation5)*:

5.   i. CASIMIR (JEAN PIERRE) GUILLEMAND[5] PINEL
(Louis Dupuy[4], Philippe François Escribe[3], Barthelemí Oliene[2],
Scipion) was born on 16 July 1800 in Tarn, Midi-Pyrénées,
France. He died on 05 December 1866 in Neuilly-sur-Seine,
France.

5.   ii.   JEAN MAURICE SCIPION GUILLEMAND[5]
PINEL (Louis Dupuy[4], Philippe François Escribe[3], Barthelemí
Oliene[2], Scipion) was born on 02 November 1792 in Saint
Paul-Cap-de-Joux, Tarn FR.

Baptized November 4th
Son of Louis Pinel, surgeon and Louise Guillemand Pinel
Godfather: Jean Pinel, of Barbet
Godmother: Jeanne Marie Pinel, sister
Temoin/Witness: Philippe Pinel, grandfather and François
Bourrel

4.   JEAN PIERRE DUPUY[4] PINEL (Philippe François Escribe[3], Barthelemí Oliene[2], Scipion[1]) was born on 07 Oct 1755 in Saint-Paul-Cap-de-Joux, France. He married MARIANNE OULIAC.

> Baptism Notes:
> Godfather: Jean Durand
> Godmother: Élisabeth Lafend

> Jean Pierre Dupuy Pinel and Marianne Ouliac had the following children *(generation5):*

5.   i.   JEAN PIERRE OULIAC[5] PINEL (Jean Pierre Dupuy[4], Philippe François Escribe[3], Barthelemí Oliene[2], Scipion) was born in 1790 in Saint Paul-Cap-de-Joux, Tarn FR.

5.   ii.   LOUIS OULIAC[5] PINEL (Jean Pierre Dupuy[4], Philippe François Escribe[3], Barthelemí Oliene[2], Scipion) was born on 17 September 1792 in Saint Paul-Cap-de-Joux, Tarn FR.

> Baptism Notes:
> Godfather: Louis Moreau
> Godmother: Jeanne Bastie

5

JEANNE FRANÇOISE VINCENT
And Her Ancestors

VINCENT-PATRUS

1.   **FRANÇOIS[1] VINCENT** was born about 1668. He married **CLAIRE CHARRIERE**. She was born in 1673 in Saint-Paul-Cap-de-Joux, France. She died in 1723.

François Vincent and Claire Charriere had the following child:

2.   i. **DESIRE[2] VINCENT** was born between 1699-1700 in Saint-Paul-Cap-de-Joux, France. He died in 1750. He married **FRANÇOISE PATRUS**. She was born in 1705 in Saint-Paul-Cap-de-Joux, France. She died in 1766.

Generation 2

2.   **DESIRE[2] VINCENT** (François[1]) was born between 1699-1700 in Saint-Paul-Cap-de-Joux, France. He died in 1750. He married **FRANÇOISE PATRUS**, daughter of **JEAN PATRUS** (born 1676 in Gevingey, Jura, Franche-Comté, FR and died after 1734). Her mother was **DENISE JANETJEAN** (born 1681 in France and died after 1734 in Gevingey, Jura, Franch-Comté, FR) She was born in 1705 in Saint-Paul-Cap-de-Joux, France. She died in 1766.

Desire Vincent and Françoise Patrus had the following children:

3.   i. **JEAN[3] VINCENT** (Desire[2], François[1]) was born on 10

February 1727 in Gevingey, Franche-Comté, France. He married **JEANNE FRANÇOISE GINDRE**, He died before 1792.

3 ii. PIERRE JOACHIM[3] VINCENT (Desire[2], François[1])was born in 1724 in Gevingey, Franche-Comté, France.

Generation 3

3. **JEAN[3] VINCENT** (Desire[2], François[1]) was born on 10 February 1727 in Gevingey, Franche-Comté, France. He married **JEANNE FRANÇOISE GINDRE**, daughter of **ANTOINE GINDRE and JOSEPHTE MATTHIEU** on 24 November 1750 in Gevingey, Jura, Franche-Comté, France. She was born on 14 Oct 1728 in Geruge, Jura, Franche-Comté, France.

Jean Vincent and Jeanne Françoise Gindre had the following children:

4. i. PIERRE[4] GINDRE VINCENT (Jean[3] , Desire[2], François[1])

4. ii. JEAN-FRANÇOIS[4] GINDRE VINCENT (Jean[3] , Desire[2], François[1]) was born in 1748 in Saint-Paul-Cap-de-Joux, France. He died in 1798. He married Jeanne-Marie Nicolas on 23 November1784 in Macornay, 39306, Jura, Franche-Comté, France. She was born in 1758 in Saint-Paul-Cap-de-Joux, France. She died in 1813.

4. iii. **JEANNE FRANÇOISE[4] GINDRE VINCENT** (Jean[3] , Desire[2], François[1]) was born on 03 July 1768 in Geruge, Franche-Comté, France. She died in 1812. She married **PHILIPPE DUPUY PINEL**, son of PHILIPPE FRANÇOIS (ESCRIBE) PINEL AND ÉLISABETH DUPUY on 20 March 1792 in Paris, Ile-de-France, France. He was born on 20 April 1745 in Saint Andre, Tarn, France. He died on 25 October 1826 in Paris, Paris, Ile-de-France.

GINDRE

1. **LAURENT[1] GINDRE** . He married **CLAUDINE BOUILLOT.**

Laurent Gindre was born at of Geruge, Jura, France Abt 1666. His parents were Claude Gindre and Mrs. Claude Gindre.

He married Claudine Bouillot Abt 1689 at of Geruge, Jura, France. Claudine Bouillot was born at of Geruge, Jura, France Abt 1668 .

They were the parents of 6 children:

2.   i.   JEAN BENOIT[2] BOUILLOT GINDRE born Abt 1690.

2.   ii.   CLAUDE[2] BOUILLOT GINDRE born Abt 1692.

2.   iii.   **ANTOINE[2] BOUILLOT GINDRE** born 1694.

2.   iv.   CECILE[2] BOUILLOT GINDRE born 1696.

2.   v.   CLAUDE FRANÇOIS[2] BOUILLOT GINDRE christened 14 September 1707.

2.   vi.   CLAUDIA JOSEPHTE[2] BOUILLOT GINDRE christened 28 February 1711

Generation 2

2.   **ANTOINE[2] BOUILLOT GINDRE** (Laurent[1]) was born in 1694 in Geruge, Jura, Franche-Comté, France. He died on 07 December 1739 in Geruge, Jura, Franche-Comté, France. He married **JOSEPHTE MATTHIEU** on 19 January 1724 in Geruge, Jura, Franche-Comté, France. She was born in 1696 in Geruge, Jura, Franche-Comté, France.

Antoine Gindre and Josephte Matthieu had the following children:

3.   i.   JOSEPHTE[3] MATTHIEU GINDRE (Antoine[2], Laurent[1]) was born on 02 December 1724 in Geruge, Jura, Franche-Comté, France.

3.   ii.   CLAUDE BENOIT[3] MATTHIEU GINDRE (Antoine[2], Laurent[1]) was born on 26 December 1726 in Geruge, Jura, Franche-Comté, France.

3.   iii.   **JEANNE FRANÇOISE[3] MATTHIEU GINDRE** (Antoine[2], Laurent[1]) was born on 14 Oct 1728 in Geruge, Jura, Franche-Comté, France. She married **JEAN VINCENT**, son of Desire Vincent and Françoise Patrus on 24 November 1750 in Gevingey, Jura, Franche-Comté, France. He was born on 10 February 1727 in Gevingey, Franche-Comté, France.

3.   iv.   CLAUDIA MARIA[3] MATTHIEU GINDRE (Antoine[2], Laurent[1]) was born on 18 March 1730 in Geruge, Jura, Franche-Comté, France.

3.   v.   JEANNE BAPTISTE[3] MATTHIEU GINDRE (Antoine[2], Laurent[1]) was born on 25 July 1732 in Geruge, Jura, Franche-Comté, France.

3.   vi.   PIERRETTE LOUISE[3] MATTHIEU GINDRE (Antoine[2], Laurent[1]) was born on 02 May 1735 in Geruge, Jura, Franche-Comté, France.

3.   vii.   PIERRE[3] MATTHIEU GINDRE (Antoine[2], Laurent[1]) was born on 12 May 1737 in Geruge, Jura, Franche-Comté, France. He died on 09 December 1739.

Generation 3

3.   **JEANNE FRANÇOISE[3] GINDRE** (Antoine[2], Laurent[1]) was born on 14 Oct 1728 in Geruge, Jura, Franche-Comté, France. She married **JEAN VINCENT**, son of DESIRE VINCENT AND FRANÇOISE PATRUS on 24 November 1750 in Gevingey, Jura, Franche-Comté, France. He was born on 10 February 1727 in Gevingey, Franche-Comté, France.

Jean Vincent and Jeanne Françoise Gindre had the following children:

4. i. PIERRE[4] GINDRE VINCENT.

4. ii. JEAN-FRANÇOIS[4] GINDRE VINCENT was born in 1748 in Saint-Paul-Cap-de-Joux, France. He died in 1798. He married Jeanne-Marie Nicolas on 23 November 1784 in Macornay, 39306, Jura, Franche-Comté, France. She was born in 1758 in Saint-Paul-Cap-de-Joux, France. She died in 1813.

4. iii. **JEANNE FRANÇOISE[4] GINDRE VINCENT** was born on 13 July 1768 in Geruge, Franche-Comté, France. She died in 1812. She married **PHILIPPE DUPUY PINEL**, son of PHILIPPE FRANÇOIS (ESCRIBE) PINEL AND ÉLISABETH DUPUY on 20 March 1792 in Paris, Ile-de-France, France. He was born on 20 April 1745 in Saint Andre, Tarn, France. He died on 25 Oct 1826 in Paris, Paris, Ile-de-France, France.

Baptism Record for Jeanne Françoise Gindre Vincent

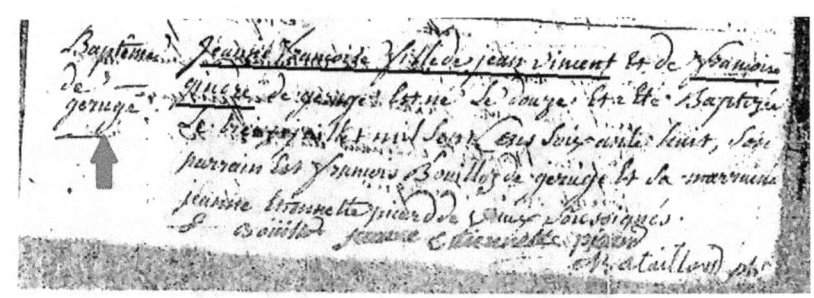

Godfather: François Bouilloz, of Geruge
Godmother: Jeanne Lhannetie

6

CHARLES VINCENT PINEL
And the next Generations

Charles Pinel

Figure 15

Generation 5

5.   **CHARLES VINCENT[5] PINEL** (Philippe Dupuy[4], Philippe François Escribe[3], Barthelemí Oliene[2], Scipion[1]) was born on 27 April 1802 in Paris, Île-de-France, France. He died on 18 July 1871 in Nova Friburgo, Rio de Janeiro, BR (Paróquia São João Baptista). He married **MARIE CATHERINE RIME**, daughter of FELIX RIME AND MARIE VERONIQUE TORNARE on 27 April 1835 in Nova Friburgo, Rio de Janeiro, BR. She was born in 1816 in Charmey, Fribourg, Switzerland (Saint Lawrence of Charmey). She died on 05 August 1890 in Nova Friburgo, Rio de Janeiro, BR.

Charles Vincent Pinel arrived 1830 in Nova Friburgo, Rio de Janeiro, Brazil

French naturalist born in Paris, 1802. Son of the famous psychiatrist Philippe Pinel (therefore he is my great-great grandfather). After graduation, he began writing plays and political articles. He was arrested for his ideas in opposition to the royalist regime. It was time to move on, so he decided to make a trip to Brazil, arriving in 1830.

Married in April 24, 1835 to Marie Catherine RIME, of Charmey.

Marie Catherine Rime Arrived 27 April 1832 in Nova Friburgo, Rio de Janeiro, Brazil

*(**see the RIMES on Chapter 8**)*

Figure 16

Until the nineteenth century some people of this family used the two forms Rime and Remy. Starting from 1850 (Law of 20.11.1849 establishing the official spelling of surnames in the canton of Freiburg) the surnames were set according to the different branches, in the manner Rime, Remy, and Remy in Switzerland. In Brazil, the family settle on the spelling Rimes.

Source: Compiled from information published in various sources, including the book by Lucy Lupia Pinel Balthazar

Charles lived in Nova Friburgo, in the state of Rio de Janeiro. There he developed a passion for botany and culture of orchids. He also gave his name to several specimens and acquired an international reputation. In 1853, the genus "Pinelia" was created by John Lindley based on the material furnished by Charles Pinel.

Source: Compiled from information published in various sources, including but not limited to the website Pinellistique (http://www.pinel.org) and the book by Lucy Lupia Pinel Balthazar

cattleya pinelli – Figure 17

From___http://purl.oclc.org/net/edu.harvard.huh/guid/uuid/53b5
71fb-b09c-4871-96ff-c0bef06a93e4

"Example of Name Published: Oncidium flabelliferum C. Pinel ex
Paxton, Paxton' s Mag. Bot. 16 : 65. 1849. Ref.: "The Frenchman,
Charles Pinel (fl. 1840s), formerly a merchant in Brazil, and Morel at
St. Mande, near Paris, were great enthusiasts; plants bearing their
names give testimony, and honor their efforts." (in Bull. Bromeliad
Soc. 4(3): 47. 1954). Eponymy: Aechmea pineliana Baker;
Echinostachys pineliana Brongn. ex Planch.; Neoregelia pineliana
L.B.Sm.; Nidularium pinelianum Lem.; Oncidium pinellianum Lindl."

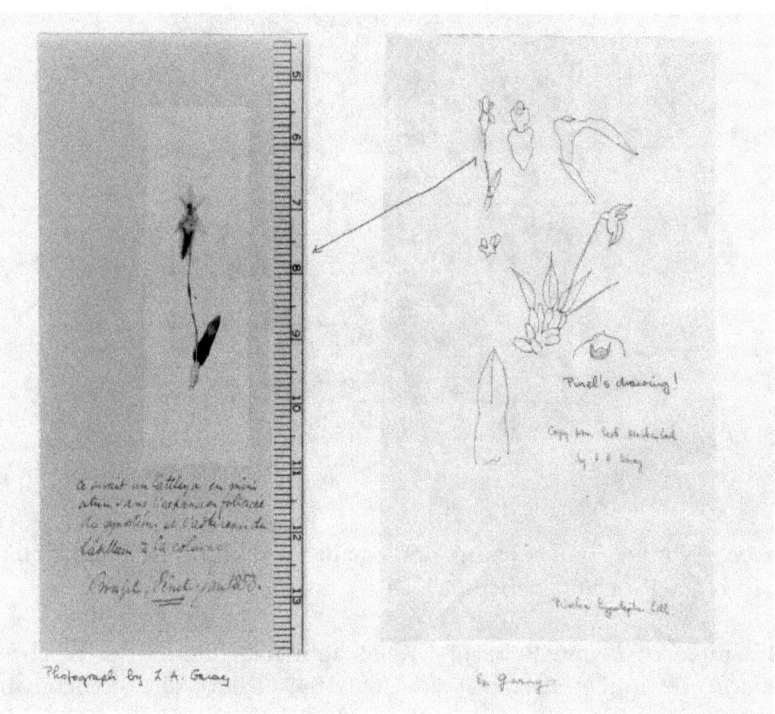

Charles Pinel's notes in January 1853

Residence: 1838 in Nova Friburgo - RJ, Brazil; Cascata Pinel (a 54 feet high waterfalls) on the shores of Rio Grande

Cascata Pinel old photo – Figure 18

Cascata Pinel today – Figure 19

They were married at Igreja de São João Baptista da Vila de Nova Friburgo.

Marie Catherine e Charles Pinel

Certidão de Casaento de Marie Catherine e Charles Pinel em 27 de abril 1835

Figure 20

Charles died in July 18, 1871.- Death Certificate
Figure 21

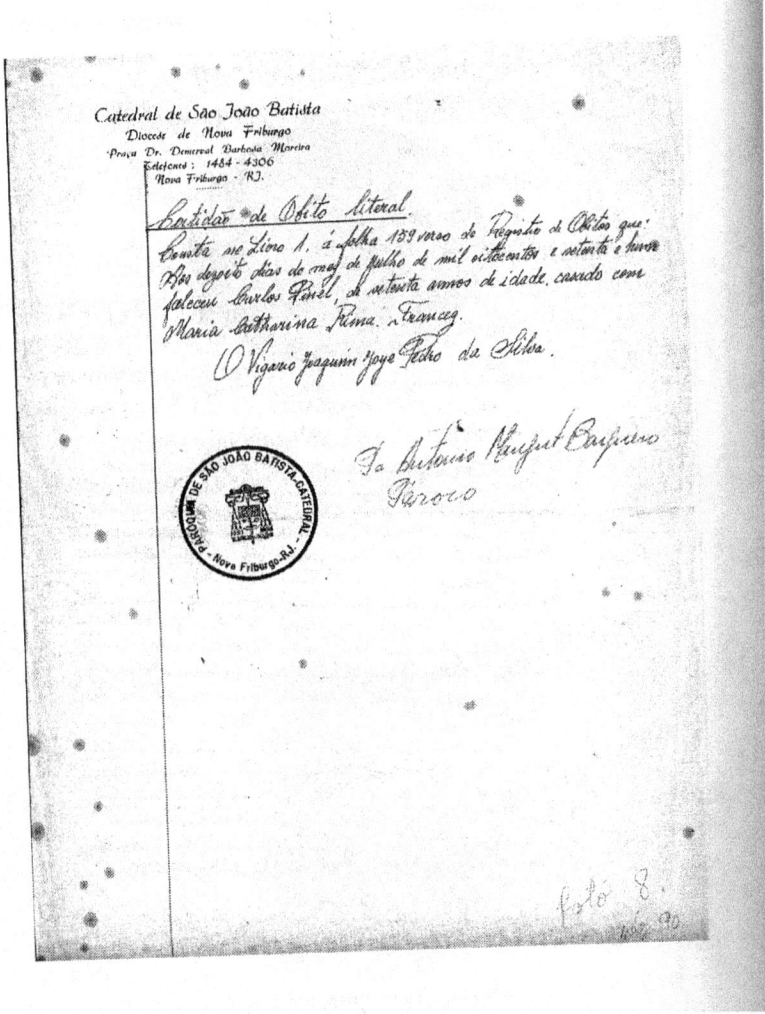

Charles Vincent Pinel and Marie Catherine Rime had the
following children *(generation 6):*

6.   i.   MARIA LEONTINA RIME[6] PINEL was born on 23
April 1837 in Nova Friburgo, Rio de Janeiro, BR. Her date of

death is unknown.

6.   ii.   CYPRIANO LUIZ FELIPE RIME[6] PINEL was born on 08 May 1841 in Nova Friburgo, Rio de Janeiro, BR. His date of death is unknown.

6.   iii.   JOANNA HONORINA AMADA RIME[6] PINEL was born on 12 March 1845 in Nova Friburgo, Rio de Janeiro, BR. Her date of death is unknown. She married Januario José Freitas. He was born in São João - Ilha Da Madeira - Portugal. His date of death is unknown.

6.   iv.   CARLOS SCIPIÃO RIME[6] PINEL was born on 22 April 1847 in Nova Friburgo, Rio de Janeiro, BR. His date of death is unknown. He married VIRGINIA DE SOUZA. She was born in 1872 in Friburgo. She died in 1938.

6.   v.   CLARA (MARIA) DOROTEA RIME[6] PINEL was born on 11 August 1849 in Nova Friburgo, Rio de Janeiro, BR. Her date of death is unknown.

6.   vi.   LUIZ LEÃO RIME[6] PINEL was born on 25 December 1852 in Nova Friburgo, Rio de Janeiro, BR. He died in 1922. He married Maria Cristina Rimes. Her date of death is unknown.

6.   vii.   AMELIA RIME[6] PINEL was born on 27 July 1854 in Nova Friburgo, Rio de Janeiro, BR. Her date of death is unknown.

6.   viii. **HENRIQUE CAMILO RIME[6] PINEL** was born on 14 July 1858 in Nova Friburgo, Rio de Janeiro, BR. He died on 29 August 1933 in Manhumirim, Minas Gerais, BR. He married **FRANCISCA RIBEIRO**. She was born in BR. Her date of death is unknown.

6.   ix.   MANOEL MEDEIROS[6] PINEL (adopted slave) was born in 1864 in Nova Friburgo, Rio de Janeiro, Brazil. He died on 25 June 1939 in Nova Friburgo, Rio de Janeiro, Brazil.

5.   SCIPION PHILIPPE VINCENT[5] PINEL (Philippe Dupuy[4], Philippe François Escribe[3], Barthelemí Oliene[2], Scipion[1]) was born on 22 March 1795 in Paris, Ile-de-France, France. He died on 17 December 1859 in Paris, Ile-de-France, France. He married HARMONIE MARGUERITE LEFEBVRE on 03 April 1824 in Paris, Ile-de-France, France (St Jean-St François). She was born in Saint-Paul-Cap-de-Joux, France. Her date of death is unknown.

Marriage Notes:
Groom: Scipion Pinel, doctor of medicine
Address: 2314 Torres, Montmartre

Parents: Philippe and Françoise Vincent (deceased)
Witness: C. Pinel, brother and J.D. Esquirol, friend

Scipion Philippe Vincent Pinel and Harmonie Marguerite Lefebvre had the following children *(generation 6)*:

6.   i.   AIMÉE DESIRÉE LEFEBVRE[6] PINEL was born in 1840 in Paris, Ile-de-France, France. Her date of death is unknown. She married EDOUARD JELES LEMIRE (LEMAIRE) on 03 May 1849 in Paris, Ile-de-France, France (St Jean-St François Parish). His date of death is unknown.

6.   ii.   CHARLES PHILIPPE LEFEBVRE[6] PINEL was born on 19 January 1828 in Paris, Ile-de-France, France. He died on 31 May 1895 in Paris, Ile-de-France, France.

5.   CASIMIR (JEAN PIERRE) GUILLEMAND[5] PINEL (Louis Dupuy[4], Philippe François (Escribe)[3], Barthelemí Oliene[2], Scipion[1]) was born on 16 July 1800 in Tarn, Midi-Pyrénées, France. He died on 05 December 1866 in Neuilly-sur-Seine, France.

Casimir (Jean Pierre) Pinel had the following child *(generation 6)*:

6.   i.   FANNY MIRA[6] PINEL was born about 1835 in Saint-Paul-Cap-de-Joux, France. Her date of death is unknown. She married ARMAND SEMELAIGNE. He was born in Saint-Paul-Cap-de-Joux, France. His date of death is unknown.

Casimir Pinel

Figure 22

5.   JEAN PIERRE[5] PINEL (Jean Pierre Dupuy[4], Philippe François Escribe[3], Barthelemí Oliene[2], Scipion[1]) was born in 1790 in Saint Paul-Cap-de-Joux, Tarn FR.

Jean Pierre Pinel had the following child (*generation 6*):

6.   i.   JEAN PIERRE[6] PINEL was born in 1815. His date of death is unknown.

Generation 6

6.   CARLOS SCIPIÃO RIME[6] PINEL (Charles Vincent[5], Philippe Dupuy[4], Philippe François Escribe[3], Barthelemí Oliene[2], Scipion[1]) was born on 22 April 1847 in Nova Friburgo, Rio de Janeiro, BR. His date of death is unknown. He married VIRGINIA DE SOUZA. She was born in 1872 in Nova Friburgo. She died in 1938 .

Carlos Scipião Rime Pinel and Virginia de Souza had the following children *(generation 7)*:

7.   i.   JULIO ZACHARIAS SOUZA[7] PINEL was born in 1895. He died on 07 July 1901 in Nova Friburgo, Rio de Janeiro, BR.

7.   ii.   MARTINHA ZILDA SOUZA[7] PINEL was born on 20 March 1905 in Nova Friburgo, Rio de Janeiro, BR. Her date of death is unknown. She married EDMUNDO PEREIRA BALTHAZAR. He was born in BR.

7.   iii.   DOMINGOS DE SOUZA[7] PINEL was born on 20 December 1906 in Nova Friburgo, Brazil.

7.   iv.   SINEZIA SOUZA[7] PINEL was born on 24 May 1908 in Nova Friburgo, Rio de Janeiro, BR. She died on 24 June 1990 in Nova Friburgo - RJ, Brazil. She married MIGUEL CANTELMO on 26 May 1931 in Nova Friburgo, Rio de Janeiro, BR. He was born on 06 February 1897 in Nova Friburgo, Rio de Janeiro, BR. He died on 15 March 1990 in Nova Friburgo - RJ, Brazil.

7.   v.   THEOTIMA SOUZA[7] PINEL was born on 18 December 1909 in Nova Friburgo, Rio de Janeiro, BR. Her date of death is unknown.

7.   vi.   JOVINIANO DE SOUZA[7] PINEL was born on 5 May 1911 in Nova Friburgo, Rio de Janeiro, BR. His date of death is unknown.

7.   vii.   CELINA CLEMENTINA DE SOUZA[7] PINEL was

born on 14 January 1913 in Nova Friburgo, Rio de Janeiro, BR.

7.   viii. HONORIA CECILIA SOUZA[7] PINEL was born in BR. Her date of death is unknown. She married OSWALDO BALTHAZAR. He was born in BR. His date of death is unknown.

7.   ix. QUIRINO SOUZA[7] PINEL.

7.   x. BELMIRO SCIPIÃO SOUZA[7] PINEL.

7.   xi. ESTEVAM SOUZA[7] PINEL.

7.   xii. MAURICIO GETULIO SOUZA[7] PINEL.

7.   xiii. HERCILIA JUSTINA SOUZA[7] PINEL. He was born in 1912.

7.   xiv. ADELINA SOUZA[7] PINEL.

7.   xv. TRANQUILINA SOUZA[7] PINEL.

7.   xvi. JOÃO CARLOS SOUZA[7] PINEL.

7.   xvii. ALIPEA SOUZA[7] PINEL. She married JOÃO ALFREDO TRANIN on 27 April 1922 in Nova Friburgo, Rio de Janeiro. He was born on 30 September 1889 in Nova Friburgo, Rio de Janeiro, BR. He died on 18 June 1937 in Nova Friburgo, Rio de Janeiro, BR.

6.   CLARA (MARIA) DOROTEA RIME[6] PINEL (Charles Vincent[5], Philippe Dupuy[4], Philippe François Escribe[3], Barthelemí Oliene[2], Scipion[1]) was born on 11 August 1849 in Nova Friburgo, Rio de Janeiro, BR. Her date of death is unknown. She married MANUEL NUNES DA ROSA, date of death unknown.

Manuel Nunes da Rosa and Clara (Maria) Dorotea Rime Pinel had the following children (*generation7*):

7.   i. SILVINO PINEL[7] ROSA.

7.   ii.   JOSEFINA PINEL[7] ROSA.

7.   iii.   ERNESTA PINEL[7] ROSA.

7.   iv.   DELMIRA PINEL[7] ROSA.

7.   v.   MARIA PINEL[7] ROSA.

7.   vi.   MAXIMILIANO PINEL[7] ROSA.

7.   vii.   JOÃO PINEL[7] ROSA.

7.   viii.   AMELIA PINEL[7] ROSA.

7.   ix.   MANUEL PINEL[7] ROSA.

6.   LUIZ LEÃO[6] RIME PINEL (Charles Vincent[5], Philippe Dupuy[4], Philippe François Escribe[3], Barthelemí Oliene[2], Scipion[1]) was born on 25 December 1852 in Nova Friburgo, Rio de Janeiro, BR. He died in 1922. He married MARIA CRISTINA RIMES and date of death is also unknown.

Luiz Leão Rime Pinel and Maria Cristina Rimes had the following child (generation 7):

7.   i.   ALFREDO LEÃO RIMES[7] PINEL.

6.   **HENRIQUE CAMILO-RIME[6] PINEL** (Charles Vincent[5], Philippe Dupuy[4], Philippe François Escribe[3], Barthelemí Oliene[2], Scipion[1]) was born on 14 July 1858 in Nova Friburgo, Rio de Janeiro, BR. He died on 29 August 1933 in Manhumirim, Minas Gerais, BR. He married **FRANCISCA RIBEIRO**. She was born in Brazil and her date of death is unknown.

Henrique Camilo (Rime) Pinel and Francisca Ribeiro had the following children (generation 7):

7.   i.   MORENINHA RIBEIRO[7] PINEL was born in BR. Her date of death is unknown.

7. ii. PALMERINDA (ZINHA) RIBEIRO[7] PINEL was born in Minas Gerais, BR. She married EMILIO SEGAL. Her date of death is unknown.

7. iii. **HERMENEGILDO CAMILO RIBEIRO[7] PINEL** was born in 1902 in Cantagalo, Espirito Santo, BR. He died on 11 March 1965. He married **HILDA BARREIRO SILVA**. She was born in 1904 in Minas Gerais, BR. She died on 25 March 1955 in Lajinha, Minas Gerais, BR.

7. iv. CARLOS ALADIM RIBEIRO[7] PINEL was born in BR. He married CAROLINA CAMPOS. His date of death is unknown.

7. v. MARIA DA GLORIA (ZICA) RIBEIRO[7] PINEL was born on 24 April1 898 in Manhumirim, Minas Gerais, BR. Her date of death is unknown. She married LUIZ ANTONIO HOTT on 03 February 1913 in Manhumirim, Minas Gerais. He was born in Manhuaçu, Minas Gerais, BR. He died on 10 February 1969 in Ocidente, Minas Gerais, BR.

7. vi. SEBASTIÃO (ZITO) RIBEIRO[7] PINEL was born in BR. His date of death is unknown.

7. vii. ZUZA RIBEIRO[7] PINEL was born in BR. His date of death is unknown.

7. viii. UNKNOWN RIBEIRO[7] PINEL.

6. AIMÉE DESIRÉE[6] PINEL (Scipion Philippe Vincent[5], Philippe Dupuy[4], Philippe François Escribe[3], Barthelemí Oliene[2], Scipion[1]) was born in 1840 in Paris, Ile-de-France, France. Her date of death is unknown. She married EDOUARD JULES LEMIRE (LEMAIRE) on 03 May 1849 in Paris, Ile-de-France, France (St Jean-St François Parish). His date of death is unknown.

> Marriage Notes:
> Parents of groom: Jean Baptist Lemaire and Margueritte Julie Closter Robart

Edouard Jules Lemire (Lemaire) and Aimée Desirée Pinel had the following child (*generation 7*):

7. i. JULES EDOUARD[7] LEMIRE was born on 06 November 1861 in Favières, Seine-et-Marne. His date of death is unknown. He married MARIE CATHERINE BENOIT MILANI on 17 July 1890 in Paris, Ile-de-France, France. She was born in Saint-Paul-Cap-de-Joux, France

6. FANNY MIRA[6] PINEL (Casimir (Jean Pierre)[5], Louis Dupuy[4], Philippe François Escribe[3], Barthelemí Oliene[2], Scipion[1]) was born about 1835 in Saint-Paul-Cap-de-Joux, France. Her date of death is unknown. She married ARMAND SEMELAIGNE. He was born in Saint-Paul-Cap-de-Joux, France. His date of death is unknown.

Armand Semelaigne and Fanny Mira Pinel had the following children (*generation 7*):

7. i. FERNAND PINEL[7] SEMELAIGNE was born about 1866 in Saint-Paul-Cap-de-Joux, France. His date of death is unknown.

7. ii. CASIMIR PINEL[7] SEMELAIGNE was born about 1854 in Saint-Paul-Cap-de-Joux, France. His date of death is unknown.

7. iii. RENE PINEL[7] SEMELAIGNE was born on 12 December 1855 in Neuilly-sur-Seine, France. He died on 16 November 1934.

6. JEAN PIERRE[6] PINEL (Jean Pierre[5], Jean Pierre Dupuy[4], Philippe François Escribe[3], Barthelemí Oliene[2], Scipion[1]) was born in 1815. His date of death is unknown.

Jean Pierre Pinel had the following child (*generation 7*):

7. i. MARIE[7] PINEL was born in 1852. Her date of death is unknown. She married VICTOR LANGEVIN. His date of death is unknown.

Generation 7

7. MARTINHA ZILDA SOUZA[7] PINEL (Carlos Scipião Rime[6], Charles Vincent[5], Philippe Dupuy[4], Philippe François Escribe[3], Barthelemí Oliene[2], Scipion[1]) was born on 20 March 1905 in Nova Friburgo, Rio de Janeiro, BR. Her date of death is unknown. She married EDMUNDO PEREIRA BALTHAZAR. He was born in BR. His date of death is unknown.

Edmundo Pereira Balthazar and Martinha Zilda Souza Pinel had the following children *(generation 8)*:

8.   i.   RENATO EDMUNDO PINEL[8] BALTHAZAR.

8.   ii. ROBERTO SILVIO PINEL[8] BALTHAZAR.

8.   iii. CARLOS EDMUNDO PINEL[8] BALTHAZAR.

8.   iv. LUCY LUPIA PINEL[8] BALTHAZAR.

7. DOMINGOS DE SOUZA[7] PINEL (Carlos Scipião Rime[6], Charles Vincent[5], Philippe Dupuy[4], Philippe François Escribe[3], Barthelemí Oliene[2], Scipion[1]) was born on 20 December 1906 in Nova Friburgo, Brazil. He married ELVIRA.

Domingos de Souza Pinel and Elvira had the following children *(generation 8)*:

8.   i.   MARCIO[8] PINEL.

8.   ii. MARIA JOSE[8] PINEL.

8.   iii. ADENIR[8] PINEL.

7. SINEZIA SOUZA[7] PINEL (Carlos Scipião Rime[6], Charles Vincent[5], Philippe Dupuy[4], Philippe François Escribe[3], Barthelemí Oliene[2], Scipion[1]) was born on 24 May 1908 in Nova Friburgo, Rio de Janeiro, BR. She died on 24 June 1990 in Nova Friburgo - RJ, Brasil. She married MIGUEL CANTELMO on 26 May 1931 in

Nova Friburgo, Rio de Janeiro, BR. He was born on 06 February 1897 in Nova Friburgo, Rio de Janeiro, BR. He died on 15 March 1990 in Nova Friburgo - RJ, Brazil.

Miguel Cantelmo and Sinezia Souza Pinel had the following children *(generation 8):*

8. i. HERCI PINEL[8] CANTELMO was born on 11 December 1935. She was born on 24 September 1939.

8. ii. MARLI PINEL[8] CANTELMO was born on 12 September 1938. She married ANTONIO KLEIN DAUDT. He was born in 1937.

7. THEOTIMA SOUZA[7] PINEL (Carlos Scipião Rime[6], Charles Vincent[5], Philippe Dupuy[4], Philippe François Escribe[3], Barthelemí Oliene[2], Scipion[1]) was born on 18 December 1909 in Nova Friburgo, Rio de Janeiro, BR. Her date of death is unknown. She married MILTON SISTON.
Milton Siston and Theotima Souza Pinel had the following child *(generation 8):*

8 i. VIRGINIA LEDA PINEL[8] SISTON.

7. JOVINIANO DE SOUZA[7] PINEL (Carlos Scipião Rime[6], Charles Vincent[5], Philippe Dupuy[4], Philippe François Escribe[3], Barthelemí Oliene[2], Scipion[1]) was born on 05 May 1911 in Nova Friburgo, Rio de Janeiro, BR. His date of death is unknown. He married CELIA DE LIMA.

Joviniano de Souza Pinel and Celia de Lima had the following children *(generation 8):*

8. i. JOEL DE LIMA[8] PINEL was born in BR.

8. ii. RITA DE CÁSSIA[8] PINEL VIEIRA was born in BR.

8. iii. JOCELY LIMA[8] PINEL MALTEZ was born in BR.

8. iv. MARIA DE FÁTIMA DE LIMA[8] PINEL was born

in BR.

8.   v.   JORGE DE LIMA[8] PINEL was born in BR.

8.   vi.   JOSÉ LUIZ DE LIMA[8] PINEL was born on 20 April 1951 in Rio de Janeiro, Rio de Janeiro, BR.

7.   QUIRINO SOUZA[7] PINEL (Carlos Scipião Rime[6], Charles Vincent[5], Philippe Dupuy[4], Philippe François Escribe[3], Barthelemí Oliene[2], Scipion[1]). He married REINALDA.

Quirino Souza Pinel and Reinalda had the following child (generation 8):

8.   i.   QUIRINO[8] PINEL.

7.   BELMIRO SCIPIÃO SOUZA[7] PINEL (Carlos Scipião Rime[6], Charles Vincent[5], Philippe Dupuy[4], Philippe François Escribe[3], Barthelemí Oliene[2], Scipion[1]). He married AUREA.

Belmiro Scipião Souza Pinel and Aurea had the following children (generation 8):

8.   i.   ARLETTE[8] PINEL.

8.   ii.   VALDOIL[8] PINEL.

8.   iii.   ETEVALDO[8] PINEL.

7.   ESTEVAM SOUZA[7] PINEL (Carlos Scipião Rime[6], Charles Vincent[5], Philippe Dupuy[4], Philippe François Escribe[3], Barthelemí Oliene[2], Scipion[1]). He married (first) MARIA DE PAULA

Estevam Souza Pinel and Maria de Paula had the following child (generation 8):

8.   i.   CARLOS CELSO DE PAULA[8] PINEL.

Estevam Souza Pinel married (second) ALICE GONÇALVES and they had the following children (generation 8):

8.   ii.   ARIETTE GONÇALVES[8] PINEL.

8.   iii.   ELIETE GONÇALVES[8] PINEL.

8.   iv.   MILTON GONÇALVES[8] PINEL.

8.   v.   RICARDO GONÇALVES[8] PINEL.

8.   vi.   RENATO GONÇALVES[8] PINEL.

7.   MAURICIO GETULIO SOUZA[7] PINEL (Carlos Scipião Rime[6], Charles Vincent[5], Philippe Dupuy[4], Philippe François Escribe[3], Barthelemí Oliene[2], Scipion[1]). He married OLGA BAETA NEVES.

Mauricio Getulio Souza Pinel and Olga Baeta Neves had the following child *(generation 8):*

8.   i.   CARLOS EDUARDO NEVES[8] PINEL.

7.   HERCILIA JUSTINA SOUZA[7] PINEL (Carlos Scipião Rime[6], Charles Vincent[5], Philippe Dupuy[4], Philippe François Escribe[3], Barthelemí Oliene[2], Scipion[1]). She married OTAVIO FRANCISCO ABRANTES. He was born in 1912.

Otavio Francisco Abrantes and Hercilia Justina Souza Pinel had the following children *(generation 8):*

8.   i.   IRENE PINEL[8] ABRANTES.

8.   ii.   OSWALDO PINEL[8] ABRANTES.

8.   iii.   HILDA PINEL[8] ABRANTES.

8.   iv.   ISAURA PINEL[8] ABRANTES.

8.   v.   IRACY PINEL[8] ABRANTES.

8.   vi.   HOMERO PINEL[8] ABRANTES.

7. ALIPEA SOUZA[7] PINEL (Carlos Scipião Rime[6], Charles Vincent[5], Philippe Dupuy[4], Philippe François Escribe[3], Barthelemí Oliene[2], Scipion[1]). She married JOÃO ALFREDO TRANIN on 27 April 1922 in Nova Friburgo, Rio de Janeiro. He was born on 30 September 1889 in Nova Friburgo, Rio de Janeiro, BR. He died on 18 June 1937 in Nova Friburgo, Rio de Janeiro, BR.

João Alfredo Trannin and Alipea Souza Pinel had the following children *(generation 8):*

8. i. CECILIA PINEL[8] TRANIN.

8. ii. CARLOS PINEL[8] TRANIN.

8. iii. WILSON PINEL[8] TRANIN.

7. SILVINO PINEL[7] ROSA (Clara (Maria) Dorotea Rime[6], Charles Vincent[5], Philippe Dupuy[4], Philippe François Escribe[3], Barthelemí Oliene[2], Scipion[1]). He married GOMES.

Silvino Pinel Rosa had the following child *(generation 8):*

8. i. CLARA GOMES[8] ROSA. She married NUNES.

7. ALFREDO LEÃO RIMES[7] PINEL (Luiz Leão Rime[6], Charles Vincent[5], Philippe Dupuy[4], Philippe François Escribe[3], Barthelemí Oliene[2], Scipion[1]).

Alfredo Leão Rimes Pinel had the following child *(generation 8):*

8. i. ROQUE[8] PINEL. He married SATHLER.

7. PALMERINDA (ZINHA) RIBEIRO[7] PINEL (Henrique Camilo Rime[6], Charles Vincent[5], Philippe Dupuy[4], Philippe François Escribe[3], Barthelemí Oliene[2], Scipion[1]) was born in Minas Gerais, BR. She married EMILIO SEGAL.

Emilio Segal and Palmerinda (Zinha) Ribeiro Pinel had the following children *(generation 8):*

8. i.   AMELIA PINEL[8] SEGAL. Her date of death is unknown.

8. ii.   EMILIA PINEL[8] SEGAL was born in Minas Gerais, BR.

8. iii.   EMILIO PINEL[8] SEGAL was born in Minas Gerais, BR. His date of death is unknown.

8. iv.   ELISA PINEL[8] SEGAL was born in Minas Gerais, BR.

8. v.   AMERICA PINEL[8] SEGAL was born in Minas Gerais, BR.

8. vi.   WIGRES PINEL[8] SEGAL was born in Minas Gerais, BR.

8. vii.   HENRIQUE PINEL[8] SEGAL was born in Minas Gerais, BR. His date of death is unknown.

7. **HERMENEGILDO   CAMILO   RIBEIRO[7]   PINEL** (Henrique Camilo Rime[6], Charles Vincent[5], Philippe Dupuy[4], Philippe François Escribe[3], Barthelemí Oliene[2], Scipion[1]) was born in 1902 in Cantagalo, Espirito Santo, BR. He died on 11 March 1965. He married **HILDA BARREIRO SILVA**. She was born in 1904 in Minas Gerais, BR. She died on 25 March 1955 in Lajinha, Minas Gerais, BR.

Hermenegildo Camilo Ribeiro Pinel and Hilda Barreiro Silva had the following children *(generation 8):*

8. i.   HERGILIANO (GILI) CAMILO SILVA[8] PINEL was born on 13 July 1922 in Minas Gerais, BR. He died in 1989. He married LABIBE LOUZADA. She was born in Minas Gerais, BR.

8. ii.   **ELÇA SILVA[8] PINEL** was born on 17 July 1924 in Sao Jose do Caparaó, Espirito Santo, BR. She married

BERNARDINO AFONSO DE SOUSA on 28 Oct 1943 in Ocidente, Minas Gerais, BR. He was born on 08 March 1909 in Ocidente, Minas Gerais, BR. He died on 13 August 1969 in Rio de Janeiro, Rio de Janeiro, BR..

8.   iii.   LOURIVAL (LOLO) CAMILO SILVA[8] PINEL was born in 1926 in Minas Gerais, BR. He died in 1988. He married first EVA. He married second ZENITH ANTONIA SILVA. She was born on 03 December 1925. She died on 19 January 2000.

8.   iv.   ELZA (ZINHA) SILVA[8] PINEL was born on 17 July 1928 in Minas Gerais, BR. She married JOVENTINO GOMES.

8.   v.   ELZY (DIDI) SILVA[8] PINEL was born on 03 Oct 1930 in Minas Gerais, BR. She died on 11 April 2002 in Juiz de Fora, Minas Gerais. She married MOACYR DUARTE RIBEIRO. He was born on 01 January 1922 in Minas Gerais, BR. He died on 03 July 1978 in Juiz de Fora, Minas Gerais, BR.

8.   vi.   ELCY SILVA[8] PINEL was born on 29 November 1931 in Minas Gerais, BR. Her date of death is unknown.

8.   vii.   ELZONI SILVA PINEL was born on 11 September 1932 in Minas Gerais, BR. She married ORLANDO.

8.   viii.   ELMY SILVA PINEL was born on 19 January 1938 in Minas Gerais, BR. She died on 21 Oct 2005. She married JOSE CARLOS IGLESIAS GANDARA. His date of death is unknown.

8.   ix.   ONOFRE CAMILO SILVA[8] PINEL was born in 1940 in Minas Gerais, Brazil.

8.   x.   ELIA SILVA[8] PINEL was born on 10 July 1941 in Manhuaçu, Minas Gerais, BR. She married WALTER NANDES. His date of death is unknown.

8.   xi.   HENRIQUE CAMILO SILVA[8] PINEL was born in

1944 in Minas Gerais, BR.

8. xii. ELCIRA SILVA[8] PINEL was born in 1946 in Minas Gerais, BR. She died in 1946.

7. CARLOS ALADIM RIBEIRO[7] PINEL (Henrique Camilo Rime[6], Charles Vincent[5], Philippe Dupuy[5], Philippe François Escribe[3], Barthelemí Oliene[2], Scipion[1]) was born in BR. His date of death is unknown. He married CAROLINA CAMPOS.

Carlos Aladim Ribeiro Pinel and Carolina Campos had the following children *(generation 8):*

8. i. ORLANDO CAMPOS[8] PINEL.

8. ii. SEBASTIÃO (TIÃO) CAMPOS[8] PINEL.

8. iii. SALUSTIANO (TATA) CAMPOS[8] PINEL.

8. iv. PEQUETITA CAMPOS[8] PINEL.

8. v. LOLÓ CAMPOS[8] PINEL.

8. vi. CAROLINA CAMPOS[8] PINEL.

8. vii. MELCHIADES CAMPOS[8] PINEL was born on 29 March 1929. He died on 09 September 1996. He married AUGUSTA ROSA PEREIRA.

7. MARIA DA GLORIA (ZICA) RIBEIRO[7] PINEL (Henrique Camilo Rime[6], Charles Vincent[5], Philippe Dupuy[4], Philippe François Escribe[3], Barthelemí Oliene[2], Scipion[1]) was born on 24 April 1898 in Manhumirim, Minas Gerais, BR. Her date of death is unknown. She married LUIZ ANTONIO HOTT on 03 February 1913 in Manhumirim, Minas Gerais. He was born in Manhuaçu, Minas Gerais, BR. He died on 10 February 1969 in Ocidente, Minas Gerais, BR.

Their Marriage was witness by: Carlos Aladim Pinel and Emilio Segall

Luiz Antonio Hott and Maria da Gloria (Zica) Ribeiro Pinel had the following children *(generation 8)*:

8. i. MARIA (COCOTA) PINEL[8] HOTT was born in Minas Gerais, BR. He was born in Minas Gerais, BR. She married JUVERCINO DUTRA DA MENDONÇA.

8. ii. ADAIL PINEL[8] HOTT was born in Minas Gerais, BR.

8. iii. ACIDONÍLIA PINEL[8] HOTT was born in Minas Gerais, BR.

8. iv. ANTONIO PINEL[8] HOTT was born in Minas Gerais, BR. He died on 01 February 2012 in Minas Gerais, BR.

8. v. ALZIRA PINEL[8] HOTT was born in Minas Gerais, BR.

8. vi. ALVETA PINEL[8] HOTT was born on 02 April 1923 in Lajinha, Minas Gerais, BR. Her date of death is unknown. She married CLERES PONCIANO SILVA on 13 December 1939 in Ocidente, Minas Gerais. He was born in Minas Gerais, BR. His date of death is unknown.

8. vii. LUIZ ANTONIO PINEL[8] HOTT was born in Minas Gerais, BR.

8. viii. JOSE PINEL[8] HOTT was born in Minas Gerais, BR.

8. ix. ALAOR PINEL[8] HOTT was born in Minas Gerais, BR.

7. SEBASTIÃO (ZITO) RIBEIRO[7] PINEL (Henrique Camilo Rime[6], Charles Vincent[6], Philippe Dupuy[4], Philippe François Escribe[3], Barthelemí Oliene[2], Scipion[1]) was born in BR. His date of death is unknown.

Sebastião (Zito) Ribeiro Pinel had the following child *(generation 8)*:

8.   i.   SEBASTIÃO[8] PINEL was born in Alegre, ES, Brazil.

7.   MARIE[7] PINEL (Jean Pierre[6], Jean Pierre[5], Jean Pierre Dupuy[4], Philippe François Escribe[3], Barthelemí Oliene[2], Scipion[1]) was born in 1852. Her date of death is unknown. She married VICTOR LANGEVIN. His date of death is unknown.

Victor Langevin and Marie Pinel had the following child (*generation 8*):

8.   i.   PAUL PINEL[8] LANGEVIN was born on 23 January 1872 in Montmartre, Paris, FR (No. 13 Rue Ravignan at Place Emile Goudeau). He died on 19 December 1946 in Paris, Ile-de-France, France (Langevin died following a brief illness. The government, which had made him a grand officer of the Legion of Honor, accorded him a state funeral. His remains were transferred to the Pantheon in 1948 at the same time as those of Jean Perrin.). He married JEANNE DESFOSSES in 1898. Her date of death is unknown.

Research notes. Langevin, the second son of Victor Langevin, an appraiser-verifier in the Montmartre section of Paris, very early displayed his liking for study. His mother, great-grandniece of the alienist Philippe Pinel, encouraged this inclination; and Langevin was always first in his class from the time he entered the École Lavoisier until he left the École Municipale de Physique et Chimie Industrielles de la Ville de Paris in 1891. (The latter school was established in 1881 by Paul Schützenberger to train engineers.) Langevin's enthusiasm was aroused by his contact with the school's director and by his laboratory work, which was supervised by Pierre Curie. To further his knowledge Langevin attended the Sorbonne (1891-1893) while teaching a private course and learning Latin on his own. In 1893 he placed first in the competitive entrance examination for the École Normale Superérieure, but he did a year of military service before attending the school. At the École Normale Supéerieure he heard the lectures of Marcel Brillouin and undertook research with Jean Perrin (then an agrégé-préparateur). Langevin placed first in the competition for the aggregation in physical sciences in 1897 and left for Cambridge to spend a year at the Cavendish Laboratory with J. J.

Thomson. Under Thomson's direction, he worked on ionization by X rays, in the process discovering, independently of Sagnac, that X rays liberate secondary electrons from metals. Also while at the Cavendish he met J. Townsend, E. Rutherford, and C. T. R. Wilson: all of them soon became friends. Upon returning to Paris, Langevin established a home (1898). He had four children: Jean (b. 1899), André(b. 1901)-both of whom became physicists-Madeleine (b. 1903), and Hélè (b. 1909). Still on scholarship, he was obliged to continue to give private lessons. .... After returning to the École Municipale de Physique et Chimie Industrielles in October 1944, Langevin devoted his greatest efforts to educational reforms and to the support of his political friends. His daughter Hélène, returned from Auschwitz, sat in the Assemblée Consultative. He joined her as a member of the Communist Party-several members of which were also members of the government-in the hope of encouraging a brotherhood that capitalism had not succeeded in establishing.

Langevin died following a brief illness. The government, which had made a grand officer of the Legion of Honor, accorded him a state funeral. His remains were transferred to the Pantheon in 1948 at the same time as those of Jean Perrin.

In 1911, it was revealed that during 1910-11 Skodowska-Curie had conducted an affair of about a year's duration with physicist Paul Langevin, a former student of Pierre Curie. He was a married man who was estranged from his wife. This resulted in a press scandal that was exploited by her academic opponents. Despite her fame as a scientist working for France, the public's attitude tended toward xenophobia-the same that had led to the Dreyfus Affair-which also fueled false speculation that Skodowska-Curie was Jewish. She was five years older than Langevin and was portrayed in the tabloids as a home-wrecker. Later, Skodowska-Curie's granddaughter, Hélène Joliot, married Langevin's grandson, Michel Langevin.

http://en.wikipedia.org/wiki/Marie_Curie

7

FROM SWITZERLAND TO BRAZIL

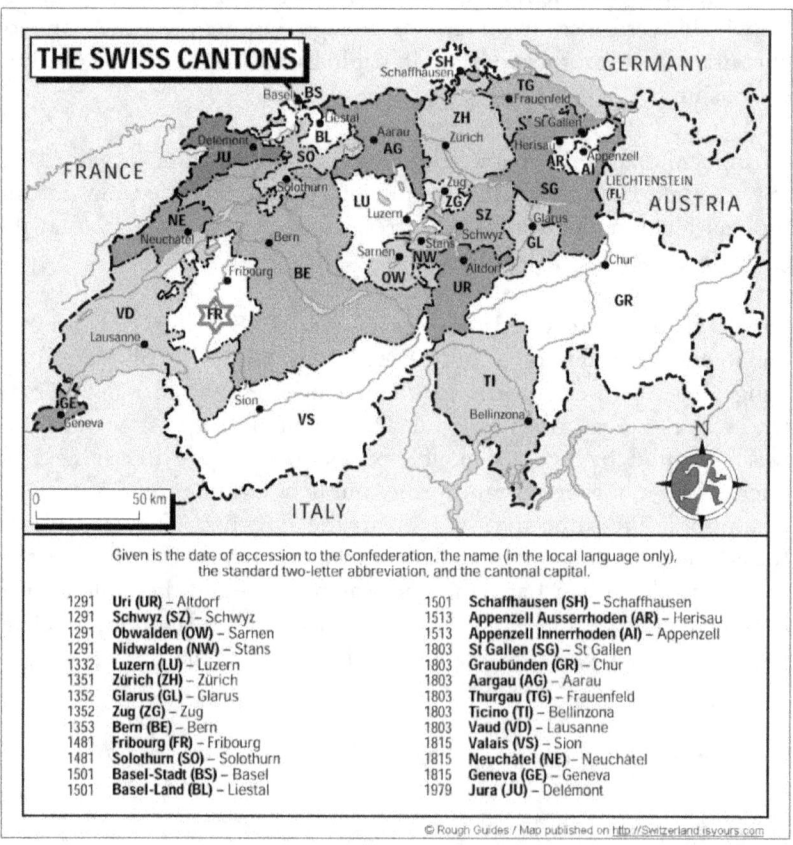

Figure 23

The Swiss Immigration -1816

During the summer of 1816, unexpected climate changes left countries in the Northern Hemisphere suffering from devastating famine and epidemic outbreaks. These weather patterns were the result of the Volcanic eruption of Mount Tambora in Sumbawa, Indonesia, on 10 April 1815.

The consequences were therefore inevitable. Thousands of Swiss leave their country and emigrate to other countries in search of better living conditions.

As Martin Nicoulin warning in his book " The Genesis of Nova Friburgo ", the migration of 1817 should not be confused with the 1816. This crisis was caused by industrial and commercial and occurred normally. The crisis of 1817 was caused by hunger and misery and had, unfortunately, death as a backdrop.

The migratory movement, from 1816, can be measured by the evolution of the economic crisis. Insofar as this deteriorates, the migration increases and take new directions.

During the summer of 1817, the French sailboat Emilie leaves the port of Le Havre toward South America. Its destination is the city of Rio de Janeiro. On board, a diplomat of Fribourg brought the commitment to an important mission. Charged by the Swiss government, its objective was to propose to the court of King João VI the delivery of a group of Swiss emigrants to Brazil.

They came from various cantons
- Argóvia
- Fribourg - 823 people
- Genebra
- Jura de Berna
- Lucerna
- Neuchátel
- Schwyz
- Soleure
- Valais
- Vaud

The voyage toward South America began on September 12, 1819, from the port of St-Gravendeel. On that date, the Hamburger sailboat Daphné , carrying 197 colonists, took the favorable wind and took the route to the ocean. The next day, left, successively, the "Urania", with 437 immigrants, of Berne, and the American "Debby Elisa", with 233 Jurasianos. A month later, the settlers remaining in Mijl, were sent to Amsterdam and from there to Den Helder. From this port left, on 10 October, "Heureux Voyage," with 442 passengers, the "Elizabeth Marie", with 228, and "Camillus" with 119 emigrants. And yet, in the first half of October, the sailboat "Trajan" leaves the port of St-Gravendeel, carrying the baggage of the settlers.

Arriving in Rio de Janeiro, the settlers did not immediately disembarked but received on board the Brazilian authorities, doctors and officials of the customs. Small sailboats led the settlers by the inside of the Bay, entering the mouth of the River Macacu and reaching Tamby (current Itambi).

In Tamby, 60 tents were erected to welcome, for 5 days, the weary travelers, the first rest ashore after months of navigation. From this village, the group left by land, with carts used to transport children, women and baggage. The men continued on foot or on horseback.

Finally, after this stage of 12 days, considered the most peaceful of the trip, ended a long journey. Of the 2,006 emigrants who left Switzerland, 1631 arrived in Nova Friburgo, being recorded during the entire journey, 389 deaths and 14 births.

The settlers who embarked in Rotterdam on the ship Urania, led by Captain Bochs on September 12, numbering 437, arrived in Rio de Janeiro on November 30, 1819 and at Morro Queimado on December 11, having lost 109 people in the crossing.

Compiled from information posted in the "Centro de Documentaçao D. João VI" Nova Friburgo, BR
http://www.djoaovi.com.br

The Urania

Figure 24

Watercolor by J. Steinmann depicting Nova Friburgo circa 1830.
Figure 25

8

RIME, RIMES OF SWITZERLAND

Hailing from various cantons of Switzerland, 2006 immigrants traveled to Brazil in order to populate the new colony of Nova Friburgo. Many, sadly, died during the long voyage.

- Argóvia
- Neuchátel
- Schwyz
- Fribourg
- Soleure

- Genebra
- Valais
- Jura de Berna
- Vaud
- Lucerna

List of immigrants from Fribourg, there were 823 people, showing Rime only:

611	Rime	Félix	35	Charmey
612		Véronique	34	
613		Marianne	7	
614		François	5	
615		Mariette	4	
616		Catherine	3	
617		Cyprine	1	
618	Rime	Jean	46	Epagny
619		Marguerite	33	
620		Marianne	7	
621		Jean-François	8	
622		Marie	6	
623		Madeleine	4	
624		Jacques	3	
625		Jean-Jacques	1	
626	Rime	Josette	26	Gruyères
627		Mariette	22	

Rhyme, Rhymes, Remy, Remy

Origin: Charmey (Gruyère County) except those of Romont.

The Rime and Remy Charmey are originally a single family. Until the nineteenth century some of the members of this family used the two forms Rime and Remy. From 1850 (Law of 20.11.1849 laying down the official spelling of the surname in the canton of Fribourg) surnames settled according to the different branches in the manner Rime, Remy and Remy Switzerland.

In Brazil the surname is set in the form Rime.

RIME RIMES: Charmey Gruyères (1633 & 1646), Cortaillod (. Nineteenth century), Geneva (1884 & 1910), Vernier (1938) Poliez Le Grand (1956), Vevey (1956), Villars-le-terroir (1956), Lausanne (1957).

REMY REMY RIMES: Charmey, Fribourg (1781), Bull (1846), Progen, La Chaux-de-Fonds (1888), Neuchâtel (1889), Le Locle (1920), Geneva (1931, 1959, 1960) Planfayon (1960), Château d'Oex (1956), and Rougemont (1958).

RIME: Romont (1951). The Rime of Romont Rataboul come from the family, aka Ratabouille

Etymology: Remy and Rimi primitives forms of this surname are popular forms of Christian name Remigius; This is St Remigius (Remy) who baptized Clovis.

Coat of Arms – Figures 26

RIME Charmey Gruyères Cortaillod, Geneva Vernier, Poliez-Le-Grand, Vevey Villars-le-Terroir and Lausanne

"Azure, a ribbon surrounded by two gold hearts and ending at the tip of a silver crescent moon"

This one is the coat of arms for our branch of the family.

RIME of Gruyères Cortaillod, Geneva (1910), Vernier, Poliez-Le-Grand, Vevey Villars-le-Terroir and Lausanne

"Cut in Quarters: 1 and 4, full of silver, with 2 and 3, azure, and a crescent moon of silver and three silver six-pointed star with a red band running across."
(Gruyérien Bulle Museum)

REMY, RÉMY, de Charmey, Fribourg, Bulle, Genève, Le Locle, Rougemont, La Chaux-de-Fonds, Neuchâtel, Château d'Oex:

"Silver with the cross of Saint Antoine extending triangular arms that widen outwards"
(AEF: Fichier armoiries)

REMY: Bulle, Progens, Planfayon:

"From sand to a growing gold peak surmounted by three silver darts feathered in gold, one set in pale and two strip and bar, in center a sphere to Croisette issuant of gold flanked by two stars " (AEF: Fichier armoiries)

There were 4 families with the last name Rime who emigrated to Nova Friburgo in 1819.

A - Descendants of Jean Rime of Gruyères
B - Felix Rime of Charmey;
C - Jean Baptiste Rime, Epagny;
D - Jean Pierre Rime (Rémy), Charmey.

A - Descendants of Jean Rime of Gruyères

<u>1st Generation</u>

1. Jean Rime was born in Gruyères, Fribourg, Switzerland. He married Marie Claudine.

Children of Jean and Marie Claudine Rime

2.   i. Marie Josette Françoise Rime was born on June 4, 1792 in Gruyères, Fribourg, Switzerland.

2.   ii. Mariette Rime was born in 1797 in Gruyères, Fribourg, Switzerland and died on Jan. 15, 1820 Macacu.

<u>2nd Generation (Children)</u>

The two sisters Marie and Mariette Rime, traveled on the boat Urania and both came to Nova Friburgo in 1819.

2 . Marie Josette Françoise Rime was born on June 4, 1792 in Gruyères, Fribourg, Switzerland,. . She married João Gonçalves Ramos on Aug. 8, 1821 in Nova Friburgo. João, son of Paulo José Vianna and Sebastiana Joaquina, was born in Barcellos, Portugal. .

Children of Marie Josette Françoise Rime and João Gonçalves Ramos (3rd generation)

> 3. i. Bernardo Fortunato Ramos was born on Aug. 20, 1821 in Nova Friburgo. .

> 3. ii Manoel Ramos was born on Feb. 9, 1823 in Nova Friburgo. .

> 3. iii. Francisca Gonçalves Ramos was born on Apr. 29, 1826 in Nova Friburgo. .

> 3. iv. José Luiz Gonçalves Ramos was born on Oct. 18, 1829 in Nova Friburgo.

> 3. v. Francisco Luiz Gonçalves Ramos was born on June 22, 1831 and died in Nova Friburgo.

> 3. vi. Maria Clemencia Ramos Gonçalves was born on Mar. 1, 1835 and died in Nova Friburgo date unknown.

2. Mariette Rime was born in 1797 in Gruyères, Fribourg, Switzerland and died on Jan. 15, 1820 Macacu.

B - Descendants of Felix Rime

1st Generation

1. Felix Rime was born in 1783 in Fribourg, Switzerland. .

He arrived on the boat Urania in 1819; New Friburgo and received Section 8 and Lot 41.

He married Véronique Tornare. Véronique was born in 1785 in Fribourg, Switzerland and died on Mar. 30, 1850 in Nova Friburgo.

Children of Félix Rime and Véronique Tornare

2.   i. Marianne Rime was born in 1812 in Fribourg, Switzerland and died on Oct. 5, 1819 on board of the Urania.

2.   ii. François Rime was born in 1814 in Fribourg, Switzerland and died on Oct. 7, 1819 on board of the Urania

2.   iii. Mariette Rime was born in 1815 in Fribourg, Switzerland and died on Oct. 5, 1819 on board of the Urania

2.   iv. **MARIE CATHERINE RIME** was born in 1816 in Fribourg, Switzerland,. .

2.   v. Cyprine Rime was born in 1818 in Fribourg, Switzerland and died on Oct. 29, 1819 in on board of the Urania

2.   vi. João Joseph Cipriano Rime was born on Mar. 10, 1821 and died in Nova Friburgo on 1st of April, 1901.

2.   vii. Jesuina Maria Rime was born on Jan. 18, 1823 in Nova Friburgo and died on May 15, 1823 in Nova Friburgo.

2.   viii. Alexander Rime was born on Dec. 29, 1823 in Nova Friburgo and died on Jan. 2, 1824 in Nova Friburgo.

2.   ix. Maria Luiza Rime was born on Aug. 24, 1825 in Nova Friburgo and died on Apr. 22, 1859 in Nova Friburgo.

2nd Generation (Children)

2. Marianne Rime was born in 1812 in Fribourg, Switzerland and died on Oct. 5, 1819 on board of the Urania

2. François Rime was born in 1814 in Fribourg, Switzerland and died on Oct. 7, 1819 on board of the Urania

2. Mariette Rime was born in 1815 in Fribourg, Switzerland and died on Oct. 5, 1819 on board of the Urania

2. **MARIE CATHERINE RIME** was born in 1816 in Fribourg, Switzerland, and died August 5th, 1890 in Nova Friburgo, RJ. She married **CHARLES PINEL** on Apr. 27, 1832 in Nova Friburgo. Charles, son of PHILIPPE PINEL and JEANNE-FRANÇOISE VINCENT, was born in 1802 in Paris and died July 18, 1871 in Nova Friburgo, RJ.

Children of Charles and Marianne Catherine Rime Pinel (3rd generation)

    3   i.   Maria Leontina Pinel was born on Apr. 23, 1837 in Nova Friburgo.

    3.   ii.   Cypriano Luiz Felipe Pinel was born on May 8, 1841 in Nova Friburgo.

    3.   iii.   Joanna Honorina Pinel was born on Mar. 12, 1845 in Nova Friburgo.

    3.   iv.   Carlos Pinel Scipião was born on Apr. 22, 1847 in Nova Friburgo.

    3.   v.   Clara Dorotéa Pinel was born on Aug. 11, 1849 in Nova Friburgo.

    3.   vi.   Luiz Leão Pinel was born on Dec. 25, 1852 in Nova Friburgo.

    3.   vii.   Amelia Pinel was born on July 27, 1854 in Nova Friburgo.

    3.   viii.   **HENRIQUE CAMILLO PINEL** was born on Jul. 14, 1858 in Nova Friburgo.

2. Cyprine Rime was born in 1818 in Fribourg, Switzerland and died on Oct. 29, 1819 on board of the Urania.

2. João Jose Cipriano Rime was born on Mar. 10, 1821 and died in Nova Friburgo. He married (first) Maria Senhorinha in Coimbra, daughter of Paulo da Costa Coimbra and Senhorinha Maria de Siqueira, on May 29, 1844 in Nova Friburgo. He married (second) Florentina Meuret, daughter of Blasius Conrad Meuret and Marianne Risset, was born in 1827 in Nova Friburgo and died on Nov. 22, 1907 in Nova Friburgo. Born in Brazil, João Jose Cipriano Rime was the only male child of Felix and Veronique to carry on the last name of this family.

Children of João Jose Cipriano Rime and Maria Senhorinha Coimbra (3rd generation)

    3.   i.   Marianna Rime was born on Aug. 8, 1846 in Nova Friburgo.

    3.   ii.   Cypriana Rime was born on May 28, 1848 in Nova Friburgo.

    3.   iii.   Antonia Rime was born on May 10, 1849 in Nova Friburgo.

    3.   iv.   Christina Rime was born on May 15, 1850 in Nova Friburgo.

    3.   v.   Pedro Cypriano Rime was born on May 13, 1851 in Nova Friburgo.

    3.   vi.   Umbelina Rime was born on Aug. 1, 1854 in Nova Friburgo.

Children of João Jose Cipriano Rime and Florentina Meuret (3rd generation)

    3.   vii.   Francisco Rime was born on Oct. 16, 1858 in Nova Friburgo.

    3.   viii.   Jose Rime was born on Jan. 10, 1860 in Nova Friburgo.

3.   ix.   Izabel Rime was born on Nov. 5, 1861 in Nova Friburgo.

3.   x.   Antonio Gaudencio Rime was born on Oct. 14, 1864 in Nova Friburgo.

3.   xi.   Joanna Antonia Rime was born on Jun. 26, 1865 in Nova Friburgo.

3.   xii.   Hermenegildo Cypriano Rime was born on Nov. 3, 1867 Nova Friburgo.

3.   xiii.   Guilerme Rime was born in 1871 in Nova Friburgo.

2.   Jesuina Maria Rime was born on Jan. 18, 1823 in Nova Friburgo and died on May 15, 1823 in Nova Friburgo.

2.   Alexander Rime was born on Dec. 29, 1823 in Nova Friburgo and died on Jan. 2, 1824 in Nova Friburgo.

2.   Maria Luiza Rime was born on Aug. 24, 1825 in Nova Friburgo and died on Apr. 22, 1859 in Nova Friburgo. She married Romualdo da Silva Machado on Jun. 23, 1847.

Children of Maria Luiza Rime and Romualdo da Silva Machado (3rd generation)

3.   i.   Antonio Machado da Silva was born on April 22, 1859 in Nova Friburgo.

C - Descendants of Jean Baptiste Rime of Epagny (Gruyere, Fribourg)

1st Generation

1. Jean Baptiste Rime was born in 1773 in Epagny, Switzerland and died in Nova Friburgo. He married Marguerite Maradan. Marguerite was born in 1786 in Epagny, Switzerland and died on board the Urania on Sept. 14, 1819.

Children of Jean Baptiste Rime and Marguerite Maradan

2.   i   Marianne Rime was born in 1810 in Epagny, Switzerland and died on Dec. 13, 1889 in Nova Friburgo.

2.   ii.   Jean François Rime was born in 1811 in Epagny, Switzerland and died in Nova Friburgo.

2.   iii.   Marie Rime was born in 1813 in Epagny, Switzerland.

2.   iv.   Madeleine Rime was born on Jan. 3, 1815 Epagny, Switzerland and died in Nova Friburgo.

2.   v.   Jacques Rime was born in 1816 in Epagny, Switzerland and died in Nova Friburgo.

2.   vi.   Jean Jacques Rime was born in 1818 in Epagny, Switzerland and died on Jan. 29, 1896 in Nova Friburgo.

2nd Generation (Children)

2. Marianne Rime was born in 1810 in Epagny, Switzerland and died on Dec. 13, 1889 in Nova Friburgo. She married Jacques Joseph Overney on Jun. 22, 1835 in Nova Friburgo. Jacques Joseph, son of Jean Nicolas Overney and Marianne Borer, was born on Nov. 19, 1807 in Fribourg, Switzerland and died in Nova Friburgo.

Children of Marianne Rime and Jacques Joseph Overney (3rd generation)

3.   i.   Maria Margaret Overney was born in 1831 in Nova Friburgo.

3.   ii.   Jose (Juquinha) Overney born on Mar. 1, 1833 in Nova Friburgo.

3.   iii.   Maria Magdalena Overney was born on June 1, 1835 in Nova Friburgo.

3.   iv.   João Jose Overney was born on Aug. 1, 1839 in Nova Friburgo.

3.   v.   Maria Élisabeth Overney was born on Nov. 1, 1843 in Nova Friburgo.

3.   vi   Francisco Overney was born on Nov. 1, 1843 in Nova Friburgo.

3.   vii.   Jacques Augustus Overney was born on Nov. 1, 1845 in Nova Friburgo.

3.   viii.   Joaquim Overney was born in Nova Friburgo.

3.   ix.   Maria Luiza Overney was born on June 1, 1848 in Nova Friburgo.

3.   x.   Marcellino (Marcel) Overney was born on Aug. 1, 1850 in Nova Friburgo.

3.   xi.   Eugenio Overney was born on Feb. 1, 1854 in Nova Friburgo.

2. Jean François Rime was born in 1811 in Epagny, Switzerland and died in Nova Friburgo.

2. Marie Rime was born in 1813 in Epagny, Switzerland.

2. Madeleine Rime was born on Jan. 3, 1815 Epagny, Switzerland and died in Nova Friburgo. She married Jean Joseph Pachoud on May 7, 1839 in Nova Friburgo. Jean Joseph, son of François Joseph Pachoud and Marguerite Equey, born in 1803 in Granges (Veveyse), Switzerland and died in Nova Friburgo.

Children of Madeleine and Jean Joseph Rime Pachoud (3rd generation)

3.   i.   Ana Maria Margarida Pachoud born on April 3, 1840 in Nova Friburgo.

3.   ii.   Jose Casimir Pachoud was born on Sept. 10, 1841 in Nova Friburgo.

3.   iii.   Luiz Pachoud was born on June 1, 1845 in Nova Friburgo.

3.   iv.   Jacques Pachoud Augustus was born on May 5, 1847 in Nova Friburgo.

3.   v.   Antonia Paula Pachoud Genoveva was born on Mar. 26, 1850 and died in Nova Friburgo.

3.   vii.   Antonio Eduardo Pachoud was born on Apr. 17, 1852 in Nova Friburgo.

3.   vii.   Maria Emilia Pachoud Josephina was born on Jan. 3, 1858 in Nova Friburgo.

2. Jacques Rime was born in 1816 in Epagny, Switzerland and died in Nova Friburgo.

2. Jean Jacques Rime was born in 1818 in Epagny, Switzerland and died on Jan. 29, 1896 in Nova Friburgo. He married Anna Maria Luiza Overney. Anna Maria Louisa, daughter of François Overney and Mary Gachet, was born on May 1, 1825 in Switzerland and died on Feb. 7, 1907 in Nova Friburgo.

Children of Jean Jacques Rime and Anna Maria Luiza Overney (3rd generation)

3.   i.   Felicité Rime died date unknown.

3.   ii.   Izabel Rime died date unknown.

3.   iii.   Marianna Rime was born in 1854 in Nova Friburgo and died on Feb. 21, 1903 in Nova Friburgo.

3.   iv.   Mary Rime died date unknown.

3.   v.   Mallanie Rime died date unknown.

3.   vii.   Hortencia Rime died date unknown.

3.   vii.   João Francisco Rime died date unknown.

3.   viii. Julio Rime died date unknown.

3.   ix.   Magdalena Rime was born in 1854 in Nova Friburgo and died on May 10, 1902 in Nova Friburgo.

3.   x.   João Pedro Rime was born in 1864. .

3.   xi.   Pedro Augusto Rime was born in 1867 in Nova Friburgo and died on Jul. 12, 1897 in Nova Friburgo.

D - Descendants of Jean Pierre Rime of Charmey

<u>1st Generation</u>

1. Jean Pierre Rime was born in 1765 in Charmey, Fribourg, Switzerland and died on Aug. 3, 1820 in Nova Friburgo. He arrived on the boat "Camillus" in 1819; given the house 4 and lot 60. He married Marianne Paquier. Marianne was born on Apr. 29, 1772.

Children of Jean Pierre Rime and Marianne Paquier

2.   i.   Marie Madeleine Rime was born on Jan. 7, 1800

2.   ii.   Marie Louise Rime was born in 1802 in Charmey, Fribourg, Switzerland and died on Dec. 9, 1819 aboard the ship Camillus.

2.   iii. Marie Felicite Rime was born on Apr. 24, 1804 Charmey, Fribourg, Switzerland.

2.   iv.   François Rime was born on Dec. 11, 1805 Charmey, Fribourg, Switzerland.

2nd Generation (Children)

2. Marie Madeleine Rime was born on Jan. 7, 1800.

Children of Marie Madeleine Rime (3rd generation)

    3.   i.   Emilia Rime was born on Apr. 23, 1821 in Nova Friburgo.

2. Marie Louise Rime was born in 1802 in Charmey, Fribourg, Switzerland and died on Dec. 9, 1819 aboard the ship Camillus.

2. Marie Felicite Rime was born on Apr. 24, 1804 Charmey, Fribourg, Switzerland,. . She married Louis Chevrand on Oct. 1, 1821 in Nova Friburgo. Louis, son of François Chevrand and Pernette Charlotte Battu was born on Mar. 17, 1794 Pregny, Genève, Switzerland.

Children of Louis and Marie Felicite Rime Chevrand (3rd generation)

    3.   i.   Luiz Antonio Chevrand

    3.   ii.   Augusto Chevrand

    3.   iii.   Joaquim Chevrand.

2. François Rime was born on Dec. 11, 1805 Charmey, Fribourg, Switzerland. He married Madeleine Hélène Genilloud, daughter of Claude Genilloud and Marie Mossier.

Children of François Rime and Madeleine Hélène Genilloud (3rd generation)

    3.   i.   Claudio Manoel Antonio Rime died in 1904 in Nova Friburgo

9

PINEL AROUND THE WORLD

Hospital Pinel – Praia Vermelha, Botafogo, RJ
Figure 27

Institut Philippe Pinel, Montréal, Québec
Figure 28

Hospital Pinel – Pirituba, São Paulo
Figure 29

Hospital Pinel in Porto Alegre, RS
Figure 30

Figure 31

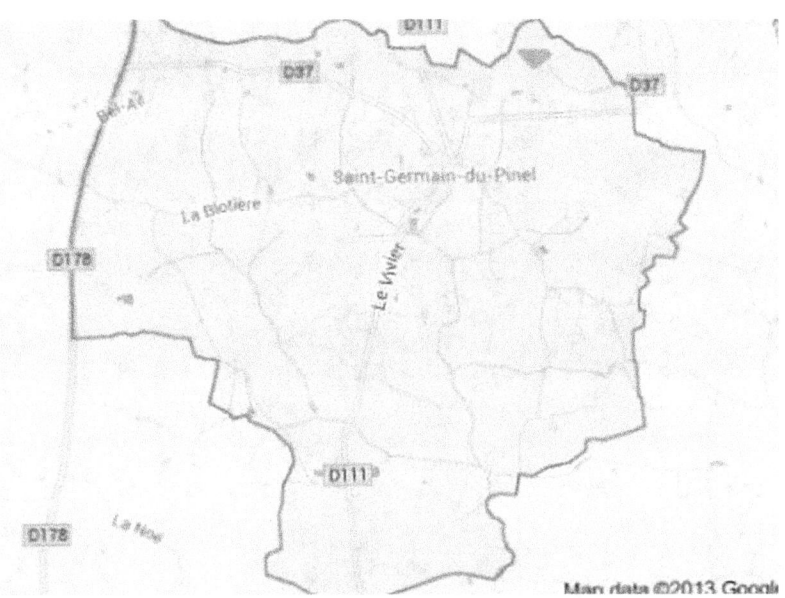

Saint-Germain-Du-Pinel
Figure 32

Pinel Island St Marteen
Figure 33

Figure 34
Pinel Island – Saint Marteen

Pinel-Hauterive, Lake Collinaire - Figure 35

10

ILLUSTRATION/PHOTOS SOURCES

1. Pinel Coat of Arms
http://tbit.ws/7924400

2. Pinel Family Name Certificate
Historical Research Center (purchased material)

3. Map of Damiatte
Google map

4. Philippe Pinel Portrait - by Anna M Merimee (d. 1852)
Paris, Musée d'Histoire de la Médecine
http://www.art-prints-on-demand.com/a/paris-musee-dhistoire-de.html

5. Bicetrê Asylum
http://www.leplaisirdesdieux.fr/Hopitaux/bicetre/

6. Engraving of Salpetriere Hospital in Paris, France. Founded in 1656
http://www.sciencephoto.com/media/300684/

7. Medal of Chevalier_légion_d'honneur
http://commons.wikimedia.org/

8. Pinel tombstone
http://cemetiereperelachaise.blogspot.com/

9. Pinel Coin
http://www.apa.org/

10. Head of Philippe Pinel, Royal Edinburgh Hospital
An image of 'the father of modern psychiatry' in the courtyard of
the old stables block in the grounds of the Royal Edinburgh
Hospital. - Copyright by kim traynor

11. Philippe Pinel Statue - Ludowig Durand, sculptor, 1885
LPLT / Wikimedia Commons

12. Pinel Stamp
http://pluq59.free.fr/

13. Pinel Street Sign
Photo by Ronilda Pinel de Sousa Shomberg - 1998

14. Philippe and Family – by Julie Forestier (1782-après 1843)
Le médecin Philippe Pinel et sa famille, 1807
Huile sur toile - 146 x 114 cm
Galerie Ladrière, 11, Quai Voltaire, 75007 Paris
Photo : Boquet et Marty de Cambiaire

15. Charles Pinel
From the book "A Historia de Philippe Pinel" by my cousin Lucy
Lupia Pinel Balthazar

16. Marie Catherine
From the book "A Historia de Philippe Pinel" by my cousin Lucy
Lupia Pinel Balthazar

17. Orchid
http://theorchidfiles.com/

18. Cascata Pinel – old
http://www.djoaovi.com.br/

19. Cascata Pinel - now a days
http://www.djoaovi.com.br/

20. Charles and Catherine Marriage Certificate
From the book "A Historia de Philippe Pinel" by my cousin Lucy
Lupia Pinel Balthazar

21. Charles Pinel death certificate
From the book "A Historia de Philippe Pinel" by my cousin Lucy
Lupia Pinel Balthazar

22. Casimir Pinel
Michel Caire, 2008
http://psychiatrie.histoire.free.fr

23. Swiss Cantons
http://www.djoaovi.com.br/

24. Ship Urania
http://www.djoaovi.com.br/

25. Water color
http://www.djoaovi.com.br/

26. Rime, Remy Coat of Arms
http://www.diesbach.com/sghcf/r/rime.html

27. Hospital Pinel – Botafogo, RJ
http://linux.an.gov.br

28. Institut Philippe Pinel – Montreal, Quebec
http://en.wikipedia.org

29. Hospital Pinel – Pirituba, SP
Pirituba.net

30. Hospital Pinel – Porto Alegre, RS
Google.com

31. St. Germain-Du-Pinel
Amazon.com

32. St. Germain-Du-Pinel map
Google.com

33. Pinel Island
www.stmartin-sxm.com

34. Pinel Island
www.stmartin-sxm.com

35. Lake Collinaire – Pinel-Hauterive
Photo by jelusa

All copies of French documents are from:
Tarn.archives
Paris.archives

<u>NOTES</u>

<u>NOTES</u>

www.ingramcontent.com/pod-product-compliance
Lightning Source LLC
Chambersburg PA
CBHW070748290526
45795CB00002B/516